Behind the headlines — the business of the British press

Behind the headlines — the business of the British press

Readings in the economics of the press

Edited by HARRY HENRY

ASSOCIATED BUSINESS PRESS
LONDON

Published by Associated Business Press
*An imprint of Associated Business
Programmes Limited*
Ludgate House
107-111 Fleet Street
London EC4A 2AB

First published 1978

© copyright Harry Henry 1978

ISBN 0 85227 213 8

Typeset by Photographics, Stockland,
Nr. Honiton, Devon.
Printed and bound in Great Britain by
Redwood Burn Ltd., Trowbridge and Esher

Contents

Introduction: What this book is about

The newspaper and magazine press of the United Kingdom employs somewhere around 400000 people, and has a turnover currently well in excess of £1500 million a year. These two facts by themselves provide sufficient justification for recognising that it is essentially a business, whatever may be thought of it as an art-form, a sociological phenomenon or a political instrument. For behind the headlines there lies a highly organised commercial structure dedicated to the task of producing and distributing more than 10000 million copies a year of over 5500 different titles (ranging from the largest mass-circulation Sunday newspaper to the smallest and most specialised professional journal) and of generating, one way or another, the revenue to meet their costs.

Nevertheless, although this large and complex industry is of direct moment not only to those who work in it and in associated industries, or who use its facilities in their own business activities, but also to a wide range of others concerned with the broader aspects of what is still the main national medium of communication, there has to date been no single source bringing together examples of the many interacting marketing factors which between them make up the pattern of the press as a whole, from which its diverse nature and present situation may be better understood and its future more clearly seen. It was this which led *ADMAP*, the monthly periodical combining in the field of advertising and marketing research and practice the functions of a professional magazine and a learned journal, to devote the bulk of its editorial space in the four last months of 1977 to a series of articles within this broad framework, and which in turn has led to their collection in this present work.

This is not to say that the press does not already receive a good deal of attention—in its own columns, in the broadcast media, from academic establishments (of various levels of competence) and some of the academics (similarly qualified) who operate in them, and even from Royal Commissions. But it is a source of perpetual irritation to anybody involved in the management of the press that such attention usually concentrates on those facets of its operations which are of little more than peripheral significance to the structure and viability of the industry and of its component enterprises.

The inadequacy of the treatment which the press as a business receives in its own columns is in part a result of the fact that the journalists who write about it have, more often than not, no direct acquaintance with the realities of management—and that by the time they have moved up into the management levels they have usually ceased to write. Associated with this is the glamour that surrounds the press, which has a dazzling effect on the vision and which encourages the perception of the market for newspapers and magazines as primarily an arena for gladiatorial combat. One typical consequence of this approach is the judgment of circulation figures as if increased sales were invariably the major marketing objective, whereas—as is made abundantly clear in more than one of the contributions to this work—the optimal level of circulation, at which any particular publication will be most stable and profitable and will best serve its market, is by no means always found by increasing sales.

Lopsided views of the workings of the press are even more

common on the television screen. In all the media of mass communication, of course, determination of the correct balance between information and entertainment presents difficulties, since in almost any situation outside the schoolroom information is only acceptable when presented in an appropriately interesting or entertaining form, but the nature of the television medium inevitably puts an even greater premium on entertainment. Thus not only fictional drama but also documentaries and news features on the press tend to concentrate on what might be termed the 'hold the front page!' syndrome, and to devote an excessive proportion of their content to the 'good television' potential of the subject—editorial conferences, journalists working on the stone, news scoops, chequebook journalism, circulation battles and the like, and of course industrial disputes. These matters are naturally not without their own importance, but they are by no means the principal constituents in determining the ability of the press to satisfy its market needs and thus operate as an efficient industry.

In a not dissimilar way, the inability of the academic to understand the functions and workings of the press is not so much a result of the manifest lack of acquaintance with how things actually happen as the consequence of a distorted approach; Lord Annan has talked about media sociologists as 'a shadowy guerrilla force on the fringes of broadcasting', and the same observation might be made in the context of the press, with psychologists being added to Marcusite sociologists as people who try to force the press into frames of reference largely irrelevant to real consumer needs.

This is equally reflected in the attitudes of politicians, and is one of the reasons why there have been three Royal Commissions on the Press in thirty years; such Royal Commissions, however, do not always do what the politicians expect of them, there being a marked inverse correlation between the integrity and level-headedness of their members and their willingness to play the required tune. The latest Royal Commission, for example, must have been a severe disappointment to the Prime Minister who appointed it, despite the inclusion of some members whose views were wholly predictable from the start and whom no amount of evidence could have persuaded that black was not white.

The contributors to the series on which this book is based, on the other hand, were selected in accordance with the not unreasonable criterion that they should know what they were talking about, from hard practical commercial experience, and within a broad general framework were encouraged to write individually on matters which they judged to be of particular moment. This has resulted in a wide variety of topics and of approaches, and, since in virtually all cases they are (or have been) involved in the day-to-day management of the newspaper and magazine press of the United Kingdom, both their choice of the particular aspects to be examined and the way in which they have opted to go about dealing with them are especially revealing of what is of particular salience in examination of the business of the press. This is not to say, of course, that so large an area can have been treated in any way exhaustively, but this is a collection of readings on the economics of the press, not a management handbook nor a surrogate Royal Commission report. And it is for this reason that a number of the articles which appeared in the original series in *ADMAP* have not been included here: they are somewhat outside the scope of this present collection, though they were highly relevant in their original context and their exclusion in no way reflects on the contribution they made there.

It may be observed, while a number of the contributors started their careers as journalists, and while questions of editorial content and its importance are referred to throughout the work, that obsession with editorial which pervades discussion of the press in its own columns, on television and radio, in academic work and in Royal Commissions, has been very deliberately avoided here. This is not to say that editorial policy is not of the greatest importance to the economics of the press—provided editorial policy is defined as the determination of what sort of content will best fit the publication for its market—but with rare exceptions the business of the press does not benefit from personality cults. Where long-term viability is sought it is the function of an editor to *execute* editorial policy, not to formulate it single-handed—he should follow the policy, not the policy him—and while it is by no means uncommon in popular mythology to ascribe the success (or failure) of particular titles to the abilities of individual editors, most of the evidence in this direction is singularly unconvincing.

One among many apparently indestructible myths, for example, is that *Picture Post* died because a particular editor was dismissed, whereas in fact *Picture Post* was only one of four almost equal-sized picture magazines all of which faded away around the same period once the post-war relaxation of newsprint rationing permitted the newspaper press to resume its pre-war functions. Books and television documentaries, therefore, about confrontations between Tom Hopkinson and Edward Hulton, though full of human interest, have no contribution to make to an understanding of why that particular category of publication disappeared, any more than the quality of their editing has anything to do with the position of the Sunday newspaper colour magazines, and it is for this reason that this sort of subject has been given no place here.

I am grateful to Admap Publications Limited for permission to republish the work which originally appeared in that publication's pages, and equally to the individual contributors, none of whom had any reason to suppose when they agreed to write a magazine article that it would eventually reappear between hard covers. Affairs sometimes move fast in the business of the press, and there is always a risk that what is written one day may be overtaken by events the next. On the other hand, changes of any real substance happen far less frequently and at a much slower rate than popular writers on the press—and broadcasters—would have us believe, and there is little in this book which has been outdated to any significant degree by subsequent developments; the sort of people who have contributed to this work do not usually finish up with egg on their faces.

My particular thanks are due to Michael Bird, Peter Clark and Norman Hart, who in addition to contributing important articles of their own acted originally as guest editors of the *ADMAP* issues covering respectively consumer magazines, regional newspapers and the trade and technical press.

H.H.

PART I

*Where the money comes
from*

1 The pattern of press revenues

HARRY HENRY

There is probably no field of business activity subject to so much heat and so little light as the economics of the press. To some extent this might be regarded as inevitable: in its combined functions as a medium of entertainment (its primary role), a medium of information and a medium of commercial communication, it is the object of a wide range of judgments where opinion is frequently undisciplined and facts usually regarded as irrelevant.

However, the doctrine that, when something is inevitable, the only rational course is to lie back and enjoy it, occasionally begs the question as to how inevitable it really is. In the case of the economics of the press, though much of the heat *is* unavoidable, the absence of light is not necessarily so, and it is important that those topics which cannot be other than matters of judgment should be set within the framework of as much factual material as is available.

The principal sources of the data here incorporated are the Advertising Association's annual review of advertising expenditure, the Business Statistics Office's *Business Monitor* of newspapers and periodicals, MEAL (Media Expenditure

	At current prices			At constant (1970) prices		
	Sales	advertising	total	Sales	advertising	total
1970	265	314	579	265	314	579
1971	306	329	635	279	301	580
1972	343	389	732	292	332	624
1973	362	496	858	282	388	670
1974	429	521	950	389	351	640
1975	530	547	1077	287	297	584
1976	614	646	1260	286	300	586

Table 1.1 The revenues of the press (£m)

Analysis Ltd) reports, and the reports of the Royal Commission on the Press. By and large these are consistent one with another in the data they produce, but dealing with minor discrepancies and the occasional lacunae has involved a certain amount of statistical art as well as statistical science: beyond this, the article is concerned not so much to reproduce existing information (though the fact that information exists does not mean that everybody is aware of it) as to transform it in such a way that its significance can be more fully appreciated.

The total revenue of the newspaper and periodical press in 1976 was £1260 million; slightly over half of this came from advertising, and slightly under half from copy sales (other revenue being relatively insignificant). This figure is rather more than twice· what it was in 1970; Table 1.1 shows the pattern of growth over the intervening years. With inflation having something more than halved the value of money during this period, however, these figures are meaningless unless looked at in real terms, and the right-hand side of the table indicates what the revenues were at constant (1970) prices, the actual figures having been deflated by the Retail Prices Index. These results are illustrated graphically in Figure 1.1, where they make manifest that remarkable

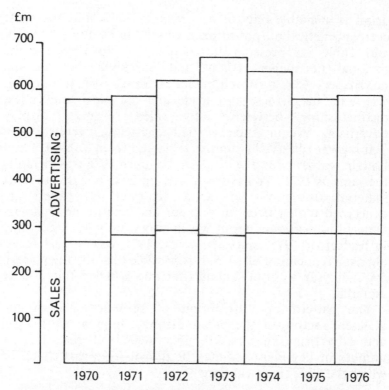

Figure 1.1 Press revenues, 1970-6, at constant (1970) prices

stability which is both so characteristic of the press and so totally unrecognised equally by the media themselves and by the advertising world. For, as can be easily enough calculated, the average variation-about-the-mean of sales revenue was only two per cent during the period, while even that for advertising revenue was no more than eight per cent, despite the cyclical swings up from the recession of 1971 to the boom of 1973 and down to the disaster year of 1975 and the saucering-out of 1976.

The press as a whole is, of course, made up of a number of different sectors, whose performances and trends do not always move in step. Information in adequately revealing detail is available only as far back as 1973, but for most current practical purposes this is enough to be going on with, and Table 1.2 presents data from 1973 to 1976 for the national newspapers (daily and Sunday), the regional newspapers (daily—which includes Sunday—and weekly), consumer magazines, and trade and technical magazines, distinguishing between copy sales revenue, display advertising revenue, and classified advertising revenue.

It may be observed from this table and from Table 1.2 that both in real terms and in its general pattern 1976 was virtually the same as 1975. This is fortunate, because one of the most material distinctions so far as national newspapers are concerned is that between popular and quality newspapers, detailed information about which is presently available only in respect of 1975: since, however, 1976 was in real terms almost a replication of 1975, it is possible to study the pattern for that year without feeling that one is using out-of-date material.

The pattern of distribution of revenue between the different sectors of the press, distinguishing between sales and advertising revenue, is illustrated in Figure 1.2. A number of key identities may be drawn from this chart, of which the most significant are:

1. National newspapers, regional newspapers, and magazines as a whole, each take about a third of total press revenue.

2. So far as national newspapers are concerned, the essential distinction is not between dailies and Sundays but between populars and qualities, advertising revenue constituting only twenty-eight per cent of total revenue in the populars but sixty per cent in the qualities.

3. Advertising provides sixty per cent of the revenue of the regional dailies, and a massive eighty-two per cent of the revenue of the regional weeklies.

4. Advertising revenue is one-third of the total revenue of

Table 1.2 Press revenues in detail, 1973-6 (£m)

		National newspapers			Regional newspapers			Magazines			Total All Press
		Daily	Sunday	Total	Daily	Weekly	Total	Consumer	Trade & Technical	Total	
Total revenue	1973	188	87	275	230	98	328	162	94	256	859
	1974	221	94	315	251	106	357	173	105	278	950
	1975	251	106	357	280	120	400	203	117	320	1077
	1976	295	124	419	320	142	462	230	149	379	1260
Sales revenue	1973	96	42	138	76	16	92	98	34	134	362
	1974	128	48	176	88	17	105	109	40	149	430
	1975	160	60	220	111	22	133	130	47	177	530
	1976	183	70	253	127	27	154	144	63	207	614
Advertising revenue	1973	92	45	137	154	82	236	64	60	124	497
	1974	93	46	139	163	89	252	64	65	129	520
	1975	91	46	137	169	98	267	73	70	143	547
	1976	112	54	166	193	115	308	86	86	172	646
Of which: Display	1973	63	37	100	61	37	98	60	43	103	301
	1974	63	36	99	64	39	103	60	46	106	308
	1975	65	37	102	72	47	119	68	52	120	341
	1976	82	44	126	82	55	137	80	66	146	409
Classified	1973	29	8	37	93	45	138	4	17	21	196
	1974	30	10	40	99	50	149	4	19	23	212
	1975	26	9	35	97	51	148	5	18	23	206
	1976	30	10	40	111	60	171	6	20	26	237

consumer magazines, but almost two-thirds of that of trade and technical magazines.

In connexion with that last point, however, two observations have to be made. The first, relating to the position of the newspaper weekend colour supplements, will be considered a little later: the second is that the 'sales revenue' of trade and technical magazines naturally includes only money which passes in the form of a cover price. That a considerable proportion of the publications in this category are 'controlled circulation' does not present any particular conceptual difficulty, more especially since there is not all that much difference between the zero sales revenue *they* get and the mere eighteen per cent obtained by the regional weeklies (which themselves include 'free sheets', accounting for some £20 million of the £98 million total advertising revenue of the category). But there are a material number of journals—*The Director* and *Management Today,* the *British Medical Journal* and the *Pharmaceutical Journal,* and so on—most of which are paid for indirectly in the overall subscription to a professional or trade association and do not show up in the 'sales revenue' statistics, even though it can reasonably be argued that a sales revenue does in fact constructively exist.

A better understanding of the general economic structure of the various press categories can be gained by considering the breakdown of advertising into display and classified, illustrated in Figure 1.3. At this point it may be noted that press advertising revenue accounted in 1975 for some sixty-nine per cent of the total of £789 million advertising revenue (net of production costs and agency commissions) of the media of communications as a whole, the balance going as twenty-three per cent to television, two per cent to directories (which in one sense are press, but are not so included here) and six per cent to outdoor, cinema and radio. The pattern in 1976 was, incidentally, substantially the same, give or take a percentage point.

Of the total advertising revenue of the press some sixty-two per cent is provided by display advertising and thirty-eight

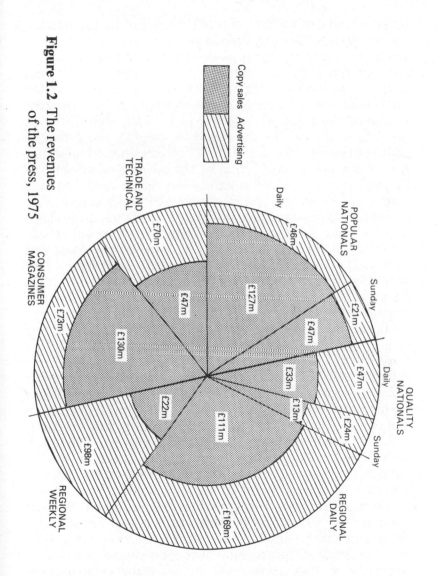

Figure 1.2 The revenues of the press, 1975

per cent by classified, but some of the differences between the various categories of publication are very sharp indeed. Once again, the distinction in the case of the national newspapers is not between daily and Sunday but between popular and quality, classified accounting for only fifteen per cent of the total advertising revenue of the former but for forty per cent of that of the latter, while it provides no less than fifty-five per cent in the case of the regionals—slightly more for the dailies than for the weeklies. That classified should not furnish a material proportion of the advertising revenue of the consumer magazines is hardly surprising, given the very long copy-dates of the large-circulation weeklies and monthlies which dominate this sector, but it might perhaps seem odd that classified revenue should constitute only about a quarter of the total advertising revenue of the trade and technical press. It could be suggested, of course, that publishers in this sector have been somewhat backward in learning the lessons of Leslie Stallard and Roy Thomson, but a more likely explanation is that a good deal of trade and technical advertising, though classified in intent, is published in display format and therefore shows up as display in the statistics.

One point to which reference has already been made concerns advertising in the quality newspaper colour supplements (in 1975 and most of 1976 divided between dailies and Sundays, but now concentrated in the Sundays). This is included, in all the statistics and in Figures 1.2 and 1.3, with the £42 million display advertising revenue of the quality nationals, of which it constituted something over a quarter. From an advertising point of view, of course, these colour supplements are essentially consumer magazines; on the other hand, if their advertising revenue were to be included in this latter sector we should have to consider whether any part of the cover price of their parent newspapers should be similarly treated, a controversial point in newspaper management theory which was discussed at some length in the January 1976 *ADMAP* and which it would be undiplomatic to raise again here.

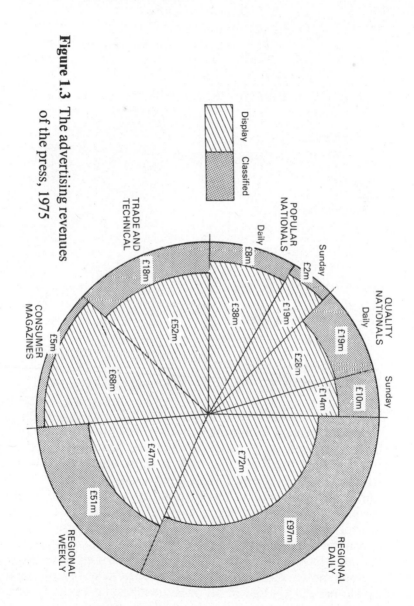

Figure 1.3 The advertising revenues of the press, 1975

	All Rev.	Copy Sales Rev.	All Ad. Rev.	Display Rev.	Classified Rev.
Total	£1,077m	£530m	£547m	£341m	£206m
	%	%	%	%	%
Nationals:					
Popular	22	33	12	17	5
Quality	11	9	13	12	14
Total	33	42	25	29	19
Regionals:					
Daily	26	21	31	21	46
Weekly	11	4	18	14	24
Total	37	25	49	35	70
Magazines:					
Consumer	19	24	13	20	2
Trade & T.	11	9	13	16	9
Total	30	33	26	36	11
	100	100	100	100	100

Table 1.3 Distribution of press revenues, 1975

The figures presented in Figures 1.2 and 1.3 may, of course, be turned round the other way to show how the three main components of total revenue are distributed between the different press sectors: this is illustrated in Table 1.3, which underlines the variations in revenue mix. For while the popular nationals take thirty-three per cent of all copy sales revenue but only twelve per cent of all advertising revenue and no more than five per cent of classified revenue, and consumer magazines, taking twenty-four per cent of sales revenue, have only thirteen per cent of classified revenue, the regional newspapers, with a quarter of the sales revenue, mop up almost exactly half of all press advertising revenue and no less than seventy per cent of all classified revenue.

It has already been observed that advertising provides just

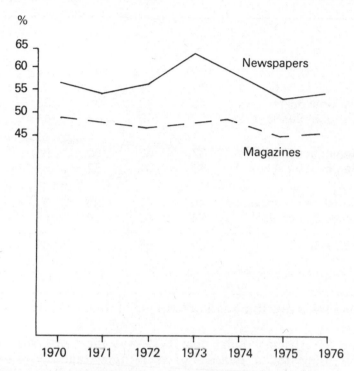

Figure 1.4 Advertising as a percentage of total revenue,
    1970-76

over half the total revenue of the press; the next issue to be
considered is what sort of trends appear to exist. It may be
noted from Figure 1.4 that while for magazines the
proportion has been gently declining since 1970, in the case of
newspapers the changes are cyclical rather than continuous.
Of course, 'newspapers' is rather too broad a category to be
particularly meaningful: the difficulty is that detailed
information for the individual newspaper sectors, at least so
far as sales revenue is concerned, is available only as far back
as 1973 (when the Advertising Association's Statistics
Working Party persuaded the *Business Monitor* to change its
format), and since 1973, as well as being the year when
double-figure inflation took off, was characterised by an all-

	1973	1974	1975	1976
	%	%	%	%
National dailies	49	42	36	38
National Sundays	52	49	43	44
Regional dailies	67	65	60	60
Regional weeklies	84	84	82	81
Consumer magazines	40	37	36	37
Trade & technical	64	62	60	58
ALL PRESS	58	55	51	51

Table 1.4 Advertising as a percentage of total revenue

time advertising boom while 1975 was the worst year for advertising for a quarter of a century (and 1976 only marginally better) the pattern shown in Table 1.4 is liable to be highly misleading as an indicator of long-term trends.

It is important to get this point right, because for a number of years addle-pated suggestions have not been lacking that the press should 'reduce its dependence on advertising'—a meaningless concept deriving particularly from the newspaper unions (who understand as little of the economics of the press as some media directors and who do not want to, since it might interfere with the rack-renting way they conduct what is laughingly called free collective bargaining). Against this background it is hardly surprising that even so relatively level-headed a body as the latest Royal Commission on the Press should have fallen into the vulgar error of regarding recent diminutions in advertising's contribution to total revenue as an encouraging sign. This would in any case not be a good thing, but in fact it simply reflects a

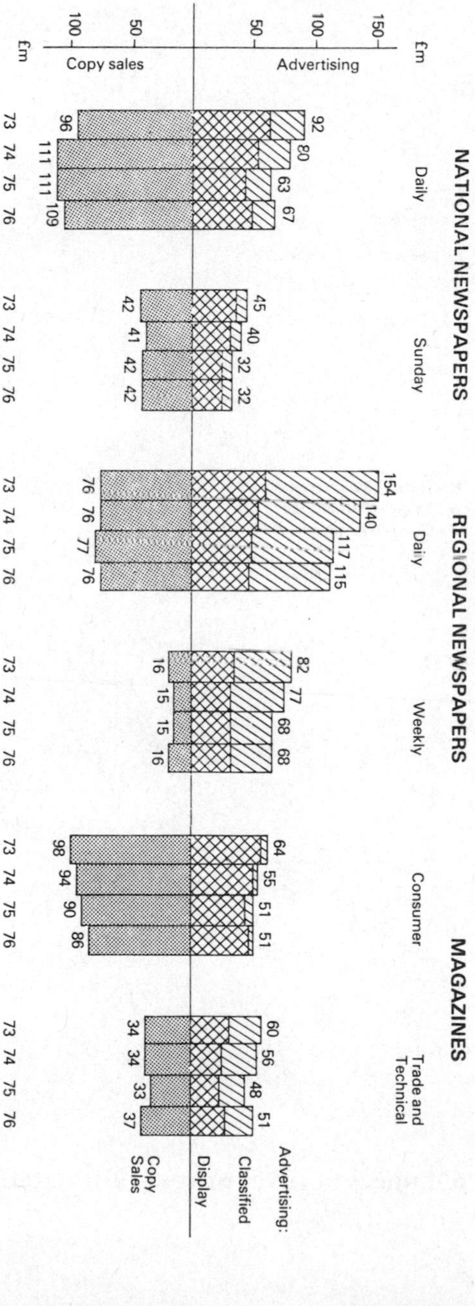

Figure 1.5 The revenues of the press at constant (1973) prices, 1973-6 (£m)

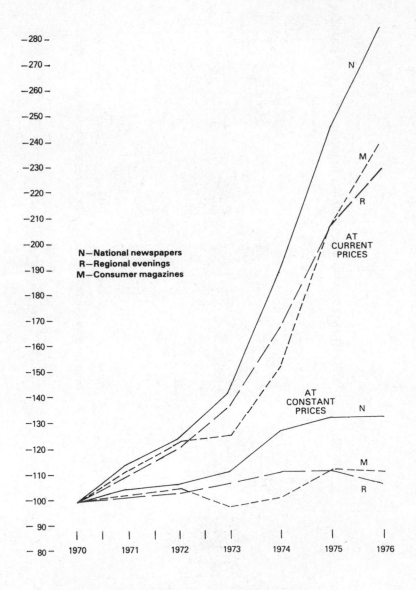

Figure 1.6 Indices of cover prices (1970 = 100)

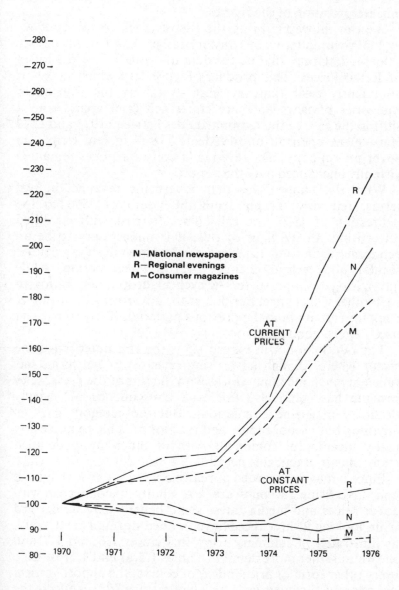

Figure 1.7 Indices of media rates (1970 = 100)

misinterpretation of the figures.

We can, however, bring the figures back to reality if we look at them in terms of constant rather than current money values—deflating, that is, the data of Table 1.2 by the Index of Retail Prices. This produces Figure 1.5, which makes it abundantly clear that, at least so far as the four main categories of newspaper are concerned (and apart from a shift in the case of the national dailies between 1973 and 1974 consequent upon an unprecedented rise—in real terms—in cover prices) copy sales revenue at constant prices remained virtually unchanged over the period.

What *did* happen was that advertising revenue, in real terms, fell very sharply from the boom of 1973 to the depression of 1975, the fall being sharpest with classified advertising. In the light of this, it is unnecessary to be an econometrician to deduce that if sales revenue shows neither secular nor cyclical changes over a given period, while advertising revenue suffers a cyclical drop, their ratios to each other will change, but that as the advertising cycle moves back into an upswing the previous pattern is likely to reassert itself. And a good thing too.

The odd man out in Figure 1.5 is the consumer magazine sector where, though advertising revenue in real terms has fallen in much the same way as with the rest of the press, sales revenue has, uniquely, fallen—a consequence of sharply declining magazine circulations. But the category itself is anything but homogenous, and it is not possible to make any really meaningful comments without much more detailed study than is practicable here.

Since it may be regarded as reasonable to suppose that sales and advertising revenues are not wholly unconnected with cover prices and media rates, some benefit may be derived from looking at how these have trended during recent years, as illustrated in summary form in Figures 1.6 and 1.7 and shown in rather more detail in Tables 1.5(a) and 1.5(b). Like every other form of price index, of course, the almost vertical direction of these curves, particularly since 1973, reflects the fall in the value of money much more than any real increases: to understand what the real increases have been it is necessary to see what the indices look like 'at constant prices', as they are shown in the lower areas of the chart. The comments which follow are in terms of these, rather than related to the actual monopoly money.

In the first place, it may be observed that while the cover prices of all three categories of publication charted were in 1976 above their 1970 levels, advertising rates (rates per thousand circulation, of course) in real terms were higher in 1976 than in 1970 only in the case of the regionals; for both national newspapers and for consumer magazines (and, indeed, the same is true for trade and technical magazines as well) they were actually lower.

The case of the regional evenings is particularly interesting, in that there is a sort of inverse relationship between changes in cover prices and changes in advertising rates, the curve for the former being convex and that for the latter concave, but the two curves coming together in 1976 at a level seven per cent above that of 1970. This suggests the existence of an unformulated trade-off theory whose existence might be regarded as reflecting more competent commercial management than is found among the nationals. On the other hand, it is probably that the regionals suffer far less than the nationals from the wholly mischievous attentions of the Prices Commission, the fundamental result of whose activities is to prevent the implementation of marketing strategies aimed at long-term viability.

Consumer magazines show a rather less consistent pattern of trade-off (hardly surprising, in view of the heterogeneity of the category), though cover prices finished up in 1976 some twelve per cent above the 1970 level and advertising rates eleven per cent down. In the case of the national newspapers, however, a more inhibited convex-concave relationship is manifest, imperfect in the very different amplitude of the curves, for while cover prices soared by 1976 to thirty-three per cent above the 1970 level, advertising rates were six per cent down.

The wisdom of matching rising costs in national

At Current Prices	1971	1972	1973	1974	1975	1976
National dailies	113	123	142	193	254	295
National Sundays	119	130	145	184	229	265
Regional evenings	110	121	137	167	207	230
General magazines	112	124	126	152	208	240
Index of retail prices	109	117	128	148	184	214
At constant prices*:						
National dailies	103	105	111	130	138	137
National Sundays	109	111	113	124	124	123
Regional evenings	102	103	107	112	112	107
General magazines	102	106	98	102	113	112

*ie. current prices deflated by the RPI

Table 1.5(a) Indices of cover prices (1970 = 100)

newspapers by cover price increases so much more than by rate increases could be accurately assessed only in the light of what is known about the relative elasticities of demand for newspaper copies and newspaper space—which is not much—and (leaving aside the problem of Prices Commission meddling) judgment in this area must be a matter of controversy out of place in what is essentially a factual review. However, it is not unreasonable to recognize that while the advertising rates of the press have doubled since 1970, as against an increase in the Retail Prices Index of 114 per cent, advertising is in fact an industrial input, and might more legitimately be compared with the Wholesale Prices Index which (as can be seen from Table 1.5b) has more than trebled since 1970.

Indeed, the difficulty facing the press as a whole in raising advertising rates to a realistic level arises as much as anything from the attitude of the advertisers, who appear to regard every rate increase as a personal insult. It is odd that large and competent manufacturing companies, who normally take

	1971	1972	1973	1974	1975	1976
At Current Prices:						
National dailies	108	111	116	138	172	203
National Sundays	107	115	120	138	161	196
Regional dailies	110	118	120	141	192	230
Regional weeklies	104	115	117	132	177	214
Consumer magazines	109	110	113	132	160	191
Trade and technical	113	119	126	145	177	211
Index of retail prices	109	117	128	148	184	214
Index of wholesale prices	104	108	141	231	252	318
At constant prices*:						
National dailies	98	95	91	93	93	95
National Sundays	98	98	94	93	87	91
Regional dailies	100	101	94	95	104	107
Regional weeklies	95	98	91	89	96	100
Consumer magazines	100	94	89	89	87	89
Trade and technical	103	102	99	98	96	98

*ie. current prices deflated by the RPI

Table 1.5(b) Indices of media rates (1970 = 100)

the view that it is bad long-term business to screw their regular suppliers into the ground, should follow such very different purchasing philosophies in the case of their advertising.

The fact that advertising rate increases have of recent years lagged so far behind cover price increases has begun to generate discussion of the relationship between the sales/advertising make-up of revenue and the editorial/advertising make-up of the newspaper itself. This latter is illustrated in Figure 1.8, in which the width of the bar

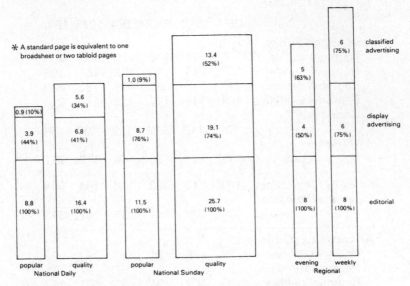

Figure 1.8 Ratios of advertising to editorial in 'average' newspapers, 1975 (in standard* pages)

for each category is proportionate to the average number of editorial pages in each, and the total area of each bar to the average total number of pages, while the percentage figures indicate the proportions to editorial respectively of display and of classified advertising. From this chart it may be seen that, within the national newspaper field, so far as display advertising is concerned the popular and the quality dailies match each other but contrast very markedly with the popular and quality Sundays (which also match each other), whereas for classified advertising the contrast is between the populars (daily or Sunday) and the qualities—also daily or Sunday, but with the Sundays carrying even more than the dailies. Within the regional field, the average weekly carries rather more advertising than the average evening, particularly display advertising—probably a function of the suitability of its smaller circulation to highly localised retail advertising.

	Advertisement pages as percentage of all pages			Advertisement revenue as percentage of all revenue		
	Display %	Class %	Total %	Display %	Class %	Total %
Popular nationals:						
daily	28	7	**35**	22	5	**27**
Sunday	40	5	**45**	28	3	**31**
Quality nationals:						
daily	24	19	**43**	35	24	**59**
Sunday	33	23	**56**	38	27	**65**
Regionals:						
daily	23	30	**53**	26	34	**60**
weekly	30	30	**60**	39	43	**82**

Table 1.6 Advertisement pages and revenue

Bringing together, for the newspaper press, the data from Figure 1.8 and the data from Figure 1.3 and expressing them in each case as percentages of the totals, produces Table 1.6, which shows that while, in the quality nationals and the regionals, both display and classified advertising provide a revenue proportionately greater than their share of total paging, the reverse is quite markedly the case with the popular nationals.

But this table is primarily important for what it does *not* prove. The relationship it shows has been used as a basis for the argument that, in the popular nationals, 'advertising no longer subsidises editorial—editorial subsidises advertising'. This fantastically simplistic approach, ignoring as it does all the complex interactions of newspaper economics, is also based upon the supreme fallacy that in the conditions of joint supply of which newspapers are a classic example, either of the joint products can be said to be 'subsidising' the other. A realistic approach to management accounting, involving the assessment of marginal profit on a contribution basis, disposes once and for all of this nonsense even in book-keeping terms (and also justifies the continued existence of most of the regional mornings). In the broader view, the implicit assumption that editorial pages are a benefit to the reader while advertisement pages are not is so much at variance with the realities of life that only an academic or a journalist—or one who has been the other—could seriously entertain it.

2 Sectoral changes in advertisement expenditure

PYM CORNISH

Deputy Chairman, Research Services Ltd.

Pym Cornish was educated at Marlborough, and Hertford College, Oxford, and has worked in industrial, market and economic research since 1959. As well as being Deputy Chairman of Research Services Limited, he is a Director of MEAL, and a member of the Advertising Association's Advertising Statistics Working Party.

Between 1973 and 1975 there was little change in total display advertising expenditure in national newspapers at current prices. At constant prices in a period of rapid inflation this was the equivalent of a fall of about a quarter. In 1976 and the first half of 1977 advertising in nationals at current prices increased significantly, but the increase in television expenditure has been greater. As a result, the proportion of all display advertising appearing in nationals has fallen a little further; at constant prices seasonally adjusted expenditure remains some fifteen per cent below the level reached in the second half of 1973.

The purpose of this article is to consider the probable reasons for the decline in the nationals' share of display advertising. It concentrates on the changes in the relative importance of broad product categories to total advertising expenditure during the 1973-7 period, and also on the influence of media rates. It ends with some personal views about the implications of the conclusions reached for the future of press advertising.

Information on quarterly advertising expenditure by product category is available only from MEAL (Media Expenditure Analysis Limited). Although MEAL data are subject to variation depending on the extent of discounting from published rate card rates, these variations can be shown to be quite small for the press; for television these differences vary widely, so ITCA (Independent Television Companies Association) revenue grossed up to allow for agency commission has been used as a substitute for the MEAL rate card rate estimate. These estimates have then been seasonally adjusted and converted to 1970 constant prices using the Retail Price Index (excluding seasonal foods), in order to bring out underlying trends.

Table 2.1 shows the breakdown of seasonally adjusted expenditure at constant prices for all press and television covered by MEAL between nationals, other press and television, with further details of the main components of the nationals. Table 2.2 shows that the share of consumables in total expenditure declined steadily up to the end of 1975 and has since made some recovery. As a result of the swing from consumables with high television expenditure to the financial, retail and industrial sector, with a traditionally low television expenditure, the share of television in total expenditure would of course be expected to fall. In fact between 1973 and the first six months of 1975 the decline in television's share was marginally less than would have been expected from the shift in total expenditure away from consumables. From the

£m (1970)	1973	1974		1975		1976		1977
	2	1	2	1	2	1	2	1
Total Nationals	51.9	43.3	44.4	38.3	38.2	40.8	40.7	42.8
Populars	27.5	24.5	24.4	21.8	22.6	24.3	24.4	26.3
Qualities	16.0	12.7	13.5	11.7	11.0	12.5	12.0	12.2
Supplements	8.4	6.1	6.5	4.8	4.6	4.0	4.3	4.3
Other press	41.8	36.0	37.7	37.5	35.4	36.9	37.1	38.8
Gross ITCA TV	71.8	59.9	59.0	53.5	56.5	64.2	59.4	69.9
Total	165.5	139.2	141.1	129.3	130.1	141.9	132.7	151.5
Nationals share %	31.4	31.1	31.5	29.6	29.4	28.8	29.7	28.3

Table 2.1 Advertising expenditure (press and television) at constant prices (media covered by MEAL)

second half of 1975 onwards television's share exceeded the
expected level by an increasing margin. At constant 1970
prices this excess amounted to £3.7 million in the second half
of 1975, £5.5 million in the first half of 1976, £3.6 million in
the second half of 1976 and £7.2 million in the first half of
1977. Actual expenditure was 11.5 per cent greater than the
television expenditure that would have been expected on the
grounds of sectoral changes in total advertising between 1973
and 1977.

It is clear from Table 2.2 that the swing to television has
been made up to two components. For the financial, retail
and industrial sector there has been a steady increase in
television's share throughout the period studies. For the two
other main sectors television's share tended to decline
between 1973 and 1975, and to increase quite strongly
thereafter. If a further allowance is made by excluding the
special case of financial, retail and industrial, it will be seen
that underlying demand for television weakened during 1974,
and then recovered sharply from mid-1975. Since the first
half of 1975 was affected by the television strike, the true
recovery of television is likely to have started early in 1975.

The factors which led to the decline in qualities and
supplements rather than populars among national
newspapers can now be identified. Firstly, within financial,
retail and industrial, the financial category was in steep
decline from 1973 to 1975; its television share has been rising
particularly fast, as has that of the industrial category.

These categories are of course intensive users of the
qualities. In contrast the retail category was steadily gaining
ground; its advertising mainly appears in populars and
regionals.

Secondly, by 1974-5 the proportion of television sets which
could receive colour was increasing very rapidly. The special
advantage of weekend supplements was therefore being
rapidly eroded. This point is illustrated in Table 2.3.

Why has this steady shift to television occurred in the
financial, retail and industrial sector, and why did television
increase its underlying share of all advertising from 1975

£m (1970)	1973	1974		1975		1976		1977
	2	1	2	1	2	1	2	1
Financial, retail, industries	38.2	35.3	35.2	34.1	36.3	37.8	38.1	39.7
TV share %	11	12	13	15	18	18	19	21
Share of total %	23.1	25.4	24.9	26.4	27.9	26.6	27.8	26.2
Services and durables	46.1	38.3	39.4	37.9	37.3	40.5	39.8	45.6
TV share %	32	33	32	31	36	35	39	36
Share of total %	27.9	27.5	27.9	29.3	28.7	28.5	29.0	30.0
Consumables	66.5	53.5	54.6	47.3	46.7	52.6	48.1	55.9
TV share %	74	75	71	72	72	78	73	78
Share of total %	40.2	38.4	38.7	36.6	35.9	37.1	35.1	36.9
Government	7.1	5.8	6.6	5.2	4.7	3.9	4.5	3.8
TV share %	28	29	21	31	24	33	20	32
Share of total %	4.3	4.2	4.7	4.0	3.6	2.7	3.3	2.5
Tobacco	7.6	6.3	5.4	4.8	5.1	7.1	6.7	6.5
TV share %	22	20	24	21	23	15	13	9
Share of total %	4.6	4.5	3.8	3.7	3.9	5.0	4.9	4.3

Note: the MEAL categories making up services are—entertainment, travel, publishing durables—household appliances and equipment, leisure equipment, motors and wearing apparel; consumables—drink, food, household stores, pharmaceutical and toiletries; government is taken together with charity.

Table 2.2 Advertising expenditure by all sectors, at constant prices (media covered by MEAL)

onwards? For the non-consumer sectors the explanation is likely to be delay in discovering the potential for television for these traditional press areas, and possibly the failure of press to respond to this challenge by exploiting fully the special characteristics of print advertising. For advertising in general the explanation is undoubtedly the sharp decline in the competitiveness of the press compared with television after the recession started. This is shown by the Advertising Association's Index of Media Rates, which is reproduced as Table 2.3 for the period 1970 to 1976.

Two columns have been added to Table 2.3 which require some explanation. The *AA Television Index* is based on changes in the average cost per advertising minute per thousand homes viewing. However, no allowance is made for the fact that the quality of an average home impression has steadily improved as the penetration of colour has increased from a negligible level in 1970 to more than half by 1976. The extra columns of Table 2.3 are an attempt to quantify this qualitative improvement. A round figure of fifty per cent increase in the value of a colour impression compared with a black and white impression is used. This may be justified on the grounds that the premium for colour in weekend supplements is about seventy-five per cent, while in women's weeklies it is about forty per cent. It is applied in the table by discounting the basic TV index by one-third of colour TV penetration in each year.[1]

In 1972 and 1973 both the AA and the adjusted TV rates moved ahead of the press rates. This satisfactorily explains the decline in the real share of television in the consumables sector during 1974. From 1974 onwards the adjusted TV series has remained over fifteen per cent behind the press series, and even with the large rate increases currently occurring the gap will not be closed during 1977. This explains the strength of demand for television from 1975 onwards and suggests that demand will remain very high for

---

[1] This matter was discussed in some detail in Harry Henry's article *Television Costs—A Few Facts* in the November 1976 *ADMAP*.

Year	Nat. Dailies	Nat. Sundays	All Press	TV	Revised TV	Penetration of colour TV %
1970	100	100	100	100	99	3.2
1971	107.7	107.1	108.6	109.0	106	7.9
1972	111.1	114.5	114.5	123.9	117	16.6
1973	116.1	120.3	118.5	136.8	124	28.9
1974	137.9	138.2	137.7	129.5	113	39.1
1975	172.4	161.2	177.5	154.9	131	46.9
1976	203.2	195.9	211.6	206.6	170	53.2

Table 2.3 AA Index of Media Rates

television relative to press throughout 1978.

What are the implications for the nationals? In the first place, although the demand for television is assured, it may not be possible to meet it. Already some television companies are preferring to hold prices and ration air time. The problem of course arises from the fixed supply of TV advertising, so that changes in demand can affect only the price rather than the volume: Hence if price is constrained in practice by either internal or external factors, demand may be diverted to other media or lost. Thus national newspapers may not in practice be affected while overall demand for advertising remains relatively firm. Their position if total demand weakens looks very vulnerable.

The second possible implication is in the creative treatment of press advertising. It is clear that the swing to television in the financial, retail and industrial sector is not simply a question of relative media costs, since it has continued steadily over the rate cycle.

A more probable explanation is therefore that television has been more successful in exploiting its special characteristics as a medium than has the press. The overwhelming advantage of press as a medium compared with television is its ability to communicate large amounts of information to self-selecting interested minorities within a total audience. Those types of advertiser in the areas of direct response and retail, have clearly found this approach rewarding. Does it not follow that the advertiser with longer term objectives should also exploit more widely the potential of press advertising to hold the attention of the interested minority? It is my impression that this was accomplished more successfully before the introduction of television than it is today.

PART II

Notes on the new technology

3 The implications of the new technology

SIR EDWARD PICKERING

Sir Edward Pickering is a director of Reed Publishing Holdings, Chairman of the Commonwealth Press Union and Vice-Chairman of the Press Council. He retired in 1977 as Chairman of Mirror Group Newspapers. He was formerly Chairman of IPC Magazines and before joining IPC was, for nearly seven years, Editor of the Daily Express.

There are three sides to every debate: your side, his side and to hell with it. The debate on New Technology is fast qualifying as a candidate for the third side.

The debate goes on worldwide. It involves publishers, editors, advertisers, printers, consultants, university dons and a whole new breed of so-called experts. Even politicians join in. The noise at times can be deafening. So before some of us lose our hearing, may I express—quietly, in old-fashioned print—a personal view on those two words, New Technology, as they apply to the national newspapers based in London.

New Technology means many different things to many

different people. Basically, it embraces three principal developments:

1. *Photo-composition* which can be a simple system of producing images on film and then using scissors-and-paste and a print-out to compose pages, or it can be a sophisticated computer-controlled system capable of full-page composition at a stroke. (More of this later.)

2. *Web-offset* printing to replace letterpress. This is a process already widely used in newspapers, but as Fleet Street still operates large letterpress plants which still have a considerable life-expectancy and the capital cost of replanting would, in present circumstances, be prohibitive, web-offset is not a priority in my considerations.

3. *Facsimile* transmission in order to facilitate multi-centre production. This again is not an immediate priority for all the national newspapers, although it is already playing a part, and might become important in future development.

So in this article, I shall confine myself to comments on photo-composition and some of its implications. First, let us look at what has been happening in recent years.

Fifteen years ago you could visit any newspaper in the world and, with minor variations, the method of production was identical. The impressive, Victorian, clanking composing machine may have been Intertype or Linotype: the presses may have been Hoe-Crabtree or Goss; but in essence, the technology was uniform. Leaving aside the language problem, a journalist or printer could go anywhere in the world and be completely at home. Not always so today. Perhaps never again.

To progress from this baseline of uniform technology to the concept and operation of the new composing technology, a number of different routes can be chosen. This underlines the fact that the choice of equipment and systems for a newspaper may now vary significantly *depending on the characteristics of the individual newspaper.*

In the United States there has been much emphasis on what is known as the 'front-end' system with terminals in editorial and advertisement departments linked, with wire-services and outside contributors, to a central computer. The computer then feeds a typesetter, producing galleys of type that can be fixed to a base-sheet and made up into a newspaper. For the newspaper with a high volume of classified advertising and a heavy editorial coverage largely relying on wire services, the 'front-end' system works admirably.

London however, with its unique competitive situation and its own trade union problems, is not the United States. The 'front-end' system may have some application to *The Times,* the *Telegraph,* the *Guardian* and *The Financial Times.* But what of the tabloids—the *Mirror, Sun, Express* and *Mail?* Four newspapers ranging in size from twenty-four to forty-eight pages: with comparatively low classified advertising volume; and an editorial presentation that relies heavily on good graphics techniques combined with tightly-written news and features. Bearing these considerations in mind, I believe that the high standards and close control essential to tabloid newspapers require a wider degree of consideration and consultation in handling news and comment than can be obtained from one man at a terminal.

The solution that Mirror Group Newspapers had devised to meet these special problems derives logically from experience with other newspaper plants within the group. That experience began with Trinidad in 1963, continued with Belfast in 1966 and resulted in the setting-up in Glasgow in 1971 of an advanced computerised composing system for two newspapers—the *Daily Record* and the *Sunday Mail*—with the largest circulations in the world to be printed by web-offset.

So that what is happening in Mirror Group Newspapers is no leap in the dark. It is a logical extension of a technology that the company has been living with for fourteen years. Let us look briefly, therefore, at the system installed in the *Mirror's* Orbit House in New Fetter Lane.

Editorial and advertisement departments stay more or less as now. The composing room is a single unit designed to produce full pages of the newspapers ready for either facsimile transmission to the Northern office in Manchester or for conversion to pattern plates which provide the printing plates for the conventional letterpress machine room.

Full-page composition—a subject frequently discussed in the technical press as a future possibility—is already operating in the *Mirror's* new composing room and is expected to be in regular production this year. It provides a clean, sharp newspaper page, and the magnesium pattern-plate process which complements it gives the best reproduction of graphics of any plate-making process.

In spite of all the factors in mass-circulation newspapers that militate against improved quality—high cost of paper and ink, tight production schedules and high press speeds—there is every expectation that the new composing system will produce a cleaner, better newspaper.

A useful exchange of views is taking place between Mirror Group technical staff and the Print Committee of the Institute of Practitioners in Advertising so that when the new system gets off the ground, the advertising industry can take full advantage of the opportunity to provide the best possible input material.

What I have described is a solution suited to the needs of Mirror Group Newspapers. Other Fleet Street newspapers and other newspapers throughout the world will continue with their own plans for the New Technology. In some cases, such as the *New York Daily News,* they will be similar to MGN's. In other newspapers with specialised setting problems—such as *The Financial Times*—there will be a sharp divergence.

There are no right or wrong systems. The production systems of the future will be tailored more and more to the needs of the individual newspaper rather than the newspaper industry as a whole.

Fortunately, even with the widest divergence, this should not cause fundamental problems for the advertising industry, and in terms of a better product, shorter deadlines and greater economies, the New Technology must contribute to the greater well-being of an industry that stands sorely in need of technological development and support.

4 Technology and the trade unions

SIR RICHARD STOREY

Chairman and Chief Executive,
Portsmouth & Sunderland Newspapers Limited

Richard Storey left Cambridge University in 1961 having obtained a BA and LLB. In 1962 he qualified as a barrister and practised as such until 1969. In 1962 he joined the Board of Portsmouth and Sunderland Newspapers Limited and became its Vice-Chairman and Chief Executive in 1969. In 1973 he became Chairman and retained the position of Chief Executive. Portsmouth and Sunderland Newspapers Limited is a medium sized provincial newspaper company with three evening newspapers and five weekly newspapers.

The methods now used for producing all except two or three provincial newspapers in this country are about ten years behind those used in many other parts of the world. The reasons for our shameful inefficiency in newspaper production are, on the one hand, trade union resistance to the new technology and, on the other, managements' indifference towards it. The consequences of this inefficiency are many: for example, higher than necessary cover prices and advertising rates and less good products for the public, maybe poorer terms and conditions for the employees and certainly lower company profits. I shall now justify these generalisations.

A leading trade unionist from one of the print unions recently wrote in *The Times* that his union was not 'refusing to accept new technology for newspaper production'. He claimed that they had 'been co-operating in the introduction of new technology in the provincial press for many years now'. That statement badly needs qualifying by some definitions.

Nevertheless, at the time of writing, there has not been a single retort of any kind to that letter from any management in any provincial newspaper nor from the Newspaper Society (the employers' association for the provincial newspaper industry). Some people believe it would be 'provocative' to tell the public about our problems. Others say 'it is not the right time', and a representative of one large group recently referred to 'photocomposition' as 'new technology' and argues the union leader's case for him.

Managements seem to see little point in involving the public in the problems of newspaper production and are prepared to leave the giving of information to the public in the hands of the trade unions. I believe this is basically wrong and that the pressure of 'opinion formers' is an important weapon in persuading all people to adopt reasonable and responsible attitudes. The power of a letter in *The Times* has been proved again and again to have a huge influence on the attitude of those who control our destiny. Managements' failure to react to trade union propaganda is, I think, as much as anything else to blame for the present inadequacies of our newspaper production methods.

In fact only three newspapers in the whole country have introduced and are able to make the optimum use of the most modern methods available, and they only achieved this ability by confrontation with the unions leading, in one case, to the closure of a local paper. The number of other newspapers in the provincial press which are now ready to introduce the most modern methods is minute, and the number of those actually pressing the trade unions to permit the introduction of such methods is probably not great enough to exceed counting on the toes of a two-toed sloth. Management, for the most part, is willing to live with the out-of-date methods it has got and rely, during the camouflage of an inflationary age, on raising advertising rates and cover prices in order to maintain profitability.

However, I believe that competition from television, local radio and the new methods—whereby television can reproduce the printed word either on screens or, as in Japan, on newsprint—together with the current severity of the periodic economic cycles which reduce newspaper sales and seriously increase raw material and other costs, will all combine to induce even the most antediluvian newspapers to modernise in order to maintain profitability and that a failure to do this would, before long, entail their closure.

Before dealing more specifically with the trade union response to any management initiative for modernisation, it is necessary to consider what I mean by 'the most modern methods available' and to distinguish between them and computerised photocomposition which some people still, apparently, regard as 'new technology'.

In the 1960s provincial newspapers began to introduce computerised type-setting and photo-composing. Computers began to be used to relieve the Linotype operator of his task of aligning the text and to produce a punched tape to be fed either into a traditional, but modified, Linotype or into a photosetter to produce text photographically.

As the power and speed of computers increased and their cost fell, it became possible to extend their uses; moreover nowadays they may be connected directly 'on line' to photosetters so as to eliminate punched tape.

This computerised photocomposition could today be described as 'behind the times'. Certainly it requires more staff and earlier deadlines while providing less accuracy and a less good newspaper than the more modern methods can.

The method I have described so far requires 'double keyboarding'. This means that the editorial, advertising or agency copy, already typed once, is passed to keyboarders who, typing it a second time then, with the help of computers and photosetters, produce photographic text. The elimination of this second keyboarding has been possible for about ten years, and it is this 'direct inputting' by editorial and advertising staff which, today, is what is so lamentably missing from newspaper production in this country.

A few newspapers, it should be said, have been lucky enough to be allowed by the trade unions to play with one of the toys (optical character reader) of direct inputting on a very limited and experimental basis. Some believe this may be a foot in the door which will ultimately make possible the full use of direct inputting.

The absence of direct inputting is lamentable because it means that newspapers must bear the cost of excess staff; it means that the deadlines for advertising and editorial are earlier than they need be—thereby reducing the newspaper's service to the public and the advertisers; it means that the accuracy of newspapers is less than it should be; it means that the production of the best newspapers possible—with more local news and editions with, thereby, better circulations—is out of the grasp of management.

Now, of course, put bleakly like that it is understandable for there to be a trade union reaction to staff reduction. Neither a trade union nor management would want to make a significant number of staff redundant but, in fact, with proper planning and a gradual introduction of the direct input method most provincial newspapers should be able to ensure no redundancy.

That is why and how the Newspaper Society, in the belated negotiations it is having for the introduction of direct inputting, is able to undertake there would be no redundancy. However, although one management has promised no redundancy and all such re-training as may be necessary, the trade unions have still refused to permit direct inputting.

When direct inputting is permitted it will mean that the journalists and the advertising staff—or the agencies concerned—will submit copy which will then be electronically read and passed direct to the photosetter by what is known as an 'optical character reader' or, alternatively, those others originating copy could, similarly, input direct to the photosetter by the use of a visual display unit (a television set with a typewriter attachment). Thus, you will see, a large part of the work currently done in the composing room will be eliminated.

The trade unions involved are the National Graphical Association—the membership of which is the higher skilled employees within the industry—the Society of Lithographic Artists and Engravers—again skilled people who are mainly responsible for the preparation of photographs in newspapers—and the National Society of Operative Printers and Graphical Media Personnel which is the union of less skilled staff who work in all areas. The National Union of Journalists and the Institute of Journalists are the two unions concerned with editorial personnel. The composing room staffs—those most affected—are members of the National Graphical Association which, like the other two production unions, generally have a closed shop in provincial newspaper offices. (I must emphasise in the most positive terms that the current argument raging over a closed shop in journalism and the freedom of expression in newspapers has *nothing* whatsoever to do with the introduction of new technology into these or any other newspapers. Anyone who, for motives of cementing union solidarity, seeks to confuse the two issues is deluding himself and the public.)

I ought to interpose here to say that there is other advanced technology (laser) in use in the United States which would eliminate, except for colour, much of the present process used in the reproduction and plate-making departments, currently manned by NGA and SLADE members. Another innovation in use in America is one which eliminates paste-up work after the photosetter. Both these processes are quite new even in America and are yet, therefore, of no immediate concern in this country—regrettably.

Reverting now to direct inputting I must explain that a typical composing room in a provincial evening newspaper may have some sixty members and, with direct inputting, that amount would be reduced by maybe something like thirty per cent. It seems clear that the unions oppose direct inputting in the provincial press, despite the undertakings of no redundancy, for three main reasons. First they fear that it will be adopted by the national newspapers where the ludicrous manning levels are well known and where not thirty per cent of a small number but, probably, a much bigger proportion of a larger number of staff would be made redundant—if, as is possible, a national newspaper could not, economically, give the no-redundancy undertakings offered by the provincial newspapers. Secondly, a decreasing union membership would diminish the power of a union's leaders. Thirdly, as mentioned above, close at hand there are these other technical developments which could also seriously deplete membership of the National Graphical Association, whose members work in paste-up and plate-making areas, and of SLADE in reproduction. There may also be a fourth reason which is that the introduction of new technology has been used, especially in America, as an occasion on which a general reorganisation may take place leading, through increased efficiency, to a further staff reduction. Indeed many newspapers in America seem to introduce technology for this reason alone.

You may wonder why those few managements which do want to introduce direct inputting find it so difficult to do so even if it is in the teeth of union hostility. Those three which have succeeded have all had to survive a period of intense and violent union hostility of the kind which makes the bravest of men quail. More particularly newspapers are peculiarly vulnerable to trade union hostility in whatever form it may take: they cannot hold stocks. If you do not sell Tuesday's paper on Tuesday, you do not sell it at all. Indeed if you attempt to sell Tuesday's evening paper at 6.00 pm in the evening as opposed to 3.00 pm in the afternoon again you will not sell it; thus almost all that day's revenue from cover prices and advertising will have been lost forever. Managements, when profits were easy to obtain in the past, were often only too ready to tolerate any trade union demand or restraint rather than be deprived of revenue. This, of course, was particularly so in Fleet Street where other newspapers gain circulation, often permanently, at the expense of one stopped. Today one can detect in some newspapers a stronger determination by management to look to the future's profitability rather than stare myopically at today's costing statement.

There is evidence, too, that the leaders of the print unions are ahead of their members and are taking a statesman-like attitude towards the introduction of direct inputting and other such devices and, of course, this is to be welcomed and they should be congratulated on their courage. In November 1976, a 'plan for action', a proposal for the introduction of new methods into Fleet Street, was devised by print union leaders and Fleet Street managements and, although it was rejected by the union members, intermittent negotiations are taking place with individual national newspapers. One can but be hopeful that one day such negotiations, and those being conducted by the Newspaper Society, will succeed in finding a formula which will permit the benefits of direct inputting to be shared between the public, the shareholders and the employees of newspapers.

A particular stumbling block at the moment is the possibility that in the not too distant future there may be amalgamations between some of the printing unions. While, obviously, this would strengthen any single union which emerged—to the extent that it would speak with a more uniform voice than may be the case now with several unions—I would strongly welcome such an amalgamation for it would, surely, do much to reduce the inter-union rivalries and demarcation disputes which the direct inputting methods emphasise. For example the National Graphical Association claims that, historically, typing text has been the job of its members and denies direct inputting of the text to journalists or advertising staff who, probably, belong to an editorial union or NATSOPA.

It is particularly sad that the National Union of Journalists has resolved at its recent Annual Delegates Meeting not to take any part in direct inputting until more enquiries have been made about it (despite the fact that it has been in use in America for many years.) Moreover it is ironic that the NUJ should take this attitude because, of all the unions, it is the only one which has a substantial amount to gain by the use of this direct inputting: it would mean that the control of a newspaper by the editorial staff would be greatly enhanced as they would not only be writing the text, but also be playing a large part in the handling of it thereafter. (It would also mean that exactly what editorial staff wrote would appear in the paper precisely in the form in which it was written—warts and all—or, hopefully, no warts at all!) One would have thought that this enlargement of horizons would be much welcomed by journalists who have so far tended only to see their outlets shrink as newspapers closed and circulations decreased. Also the introduction of new technology into the editorial section of a newspaper would give the staff who worked there an opportunity to benefit from increases in pay—in the same kind of way as photocomposition and computerised technology benefitted, and still does benefit, those employees working in production areas.

The problem of 'new technology' is not, therefore, about technical detail, but about how people organise themselves to meet the challenge of a highly competitive future. I suppose that, had the management and the employees in agriculture failed to take advantage of the technological developments available to them, corn would still be cut with a sickle and bread cost several pounds a loaf.

Newspaper managements must now react to the impairment of their companies' financial margins. There is not much they can do about high costs like newsprint, but composing room costs are something they can and therefore must tackle; efficient production methods may make the

difference between profitability with further expansion and
more jobs, or closure. I suggest the unions, for their part,
must accept that newspapers are operating in a harsher and
more exacting environment where the old rules and
assumptions about how far it is permissible to 'take weak
managements to the cleaners' apply no longer.

Whereas the trade unions may still be doing well in the
present with still profitable newspapers, the decrease in
profitibility has been so staggering in the last fifteen years
that the present apparent ease with which the printing
employees retain a position near the top of the wage level
league tables in the country is not likely to continue with the
current use of out-of-date production methods. It may only
be natural for a trade union member to give his union his
principal loyalty, but this narrow allegiance obscures the fact
that, unless a competitive product is produced, a well paid
and secure employment is jeopardised and future members
will face dire poverty. Unless, therefore, the goose which lays
the golden egg is properly looked after it will go off laying.

Finally, it is to be hoped that, albeit pathetically and
lamely, like an old man on two sticks edging his way across a
slippery floor, the provincial newspaper industry in this
country may be edging its way towards the introduction of
such technology as would be of great benefit to all who work
for or are concerned with provincial newspapers—not least
those who actually read or advertise in them! If there is not a
national agreement within a short time I believe that the
economic situation of individual companies will force the
managements of them to seek their own terms for direct
inputting and, failing such negotiated terms, they will have to
and will adopt the tactics of the three newspapers in this
country and those in America who have succeeded in the
introduction of the new methods only by direct and often
literally violent confrontation with the trade unions involved.

5 It is not too late — not quite

JOHN DIXEY

John Dixey began his newspaper career as a Fleet Street apprentice in 1948, became a trade union representative (FOC), then a trade union official, and, after working for the Newspaper Society, joined the Liverpool Daily Post and Echo as Assistant General Manager. In 1967 he joined Times Newspapers, became an Executive Director and in 1975 was appointed Director of the Newspapers Publishers' Association. He is currently Employment Affairs Adviser to the Institute of Practitioners in Advertising.

Hundreds of thousands of words of critical comment about Fleet Street have been included in Royal Commission and other reports, in magazine and feature articles and in news columns. Despite dire warnings that the present state of affairs in the industry cannot continue, the signs are that the inhabitants of the street of ink have not come to agreement on reform.

Harmful and unnecessary stoppages and instances of interference with production seem more frequent than ever and, if reports are true, the ducking and diving on the pay front which has characterised the industry over so many years is still taking place.

However, the title to this chapter means that it is not too late, not quite too late, for the people working for national newspapers to come to their senses within the individual houses and do something for the titles which provide them with their bread and butter, and jam and clotted cream. It must also be possible for people with energy, who recognise a market, to start new daily newspapers in London. In the US there are local papers of up to forty-eight pages broadsheet daily employing fewer than 350 people in all departments, employees who are expert at their jobs, happy, well paid—and union members!

Despite the complications and contradictions of what has often been described as the Fleet Street jungle, the ingredients for success and solutions for many of the industry's people problems are to hand—immediately to hand—for those interested and bold enough to reach out for them.

Intelligence and self-interest

My optimism is founded on the quality and high level of intelligence of most people in national newspapers, and the belief that they can be brought to recognise their mutual self-interest.

That there is this fund of intelligence cannot be denied. Many shop floor workers, including a number of FOCs, operate their own businesses—or their wives do—and they understand commercial problems very well. Isn't it interesting that shop floor workers known to be entrepreneurs—capitalists—are elected by colleagues to represent them in industrial matters?

I believe that if there was a fundamental re-thinking of the bargaining arrangements in the industry, to give exclusive responsibility for negotiation to those whose future well-

being will depend on the result, there would be sufficient
people receptive to a credible and relevant message—properly
presented and sustained—to carry through the change that is
so desperately needed. A positive change in attitudes would
bring the understanding, enthusiasm, effort, and loyalty of
newspapermen to the assistance of the newspapers they work
for.

Change in relationships

That such a sensible proposition as the Programme for
Action, designed by the Joint Standing Committee for the
National Newspaper Industry, comprising union general
secretaries and Fleet Street managing directors, was rejected
by union memberships gives the clue to the necessary
fundamental change in bargaining arrangements. If part of
the reason for rejection was a failure in communications, the
larger part must be ascribed to the gradual changes in the
structure and relationships within the unions, and the
tendency for managements and chapels to regard house negotiations as more important than national level discussions. In
the last twenty years, economic adversity, the results of house
bargaining, and union political developments have created a
situation where neither the employers' association—the
Newspaper Publishers Association—nor the trades unions
concerned, occupy the positions of influence and authority
they once held, with their members or anyone else.

The Newspaper Publishers Association has a handbook of
agreements with the unions which once meant something.
The wage rates scheduled used to represent the major part of
a worker's income. The hours, holidays and overtime
provisions were considered sacred. The dispute procedure
was in the main adhered to.

Today, gross pay is sometimes three times the scheduled
rate, and bargains have been struck on every other feature of
the agreements. Lack of respect for the disputes procedure is

shown by the significant number of stoppages which take place, and which would not if the disputes procedure was followed. How many stoppages have occurred which were officially backed from the outset?

As the Royal Commission on the Press report points out, the autonomy of chapels is a feature which is rarely found in other industries.

The disinclination of chapels to accept advice from union branch or national officers—let alone instructions—causes great difficulties for managements who have to rely on procedures written twenty, thirty or forty years ago.

Managements as well as chapels have contributed to the destruction of the national agreements and one cannot say that they have been wrong to accept independence. One cannot see the clock being put back and either managements or chapels ever again accepting fully and unquestioningly the authority of the NPA or the unions at branch and national level.

The alternative

The industry is at this moment in a twilight stage and it should consider accelerating the development of in-house relationships to the point where the management and chapels in individual houses accept full responsibility for negotiation without the constraints of an employers' association or trade union. This would be to create industrial entities within which employees would come to recognise the needs of *their* company, and would bargain accordingly.

The NPA's role in such circumstances would be significant in that it would provide advice about industrial developments and management techniques and be the repository of the industry's information on employment matters. The Association and the various unions could provide a long-stop disputes procedure.

The unions would need to give guidance to their chapels,

who seek autonomy, on how to work together with chapels from their own and other unions to their mutual benefit.

If chapels were given sufficient encouragement and independence I am convinced that comprehensive in-house negotiation in isolation form that being undertaken in other companies which might be better off, and might be worse off, is the way for the future. Once chapels are convinced it is *their* responsibility to ensure the success of *their* newspapers, self-interest would ensure they worked together and quickly discarded the small number of wreckers who are sadly present in the industry.

In this way management and chapels would be able to utilise effectively all their skills, talents, and intelligence in negotiating over the whole range of terms and conditions of employment and factors affecting the future of *their* business.

Relativities and differentials

Relativities—between one house and another—may at times seem important, but they are not a consideration for most employees compared with security of employment. I believe in-house discussions would prove this, and men would be ready to accept they could not expect to do as well as their friends in the house next door until *their* own newspapers, with *their* help, become stronger commercially.

Differentials—between categories of worker in the same house—are a problem which can only be solved by in-house discussion. More than half the industrial relations problems in Fleet Street arise from dissatisfaction with wage relationships, and no management decision or NPA/Union negotiation can ever effectively satisfy the complainants. The way to provide a lasting solution to the differentials dilemma is for in-house work groups to agree their own 'felt-fair' pecking order, using simple or more sophisticated techniques, as they wish. Then, taking into account skill, responsibility, effort, and working conditions, the work groups become responsible for agreeing the relationship of one job to another, and no job would move against another—up or down—unless the work groups agreed. Such a system is essential for the acceptable slotting in of the new jobs which will arrive with the new technology. It is easy to see that no industry job and wage relationship proposals could take account of the various factors present in the operations of individual houses.

It seems likely that the reform of wages structures, the introduction of new technology, agreement on standards of performance, and the reationalisation of manning scales, can be achieved on the basis of the management of each house and its chapels being free to negotiate with each other without interference or influence from outside.

Management initiatives

A corollary would be that having accepted with its own chapels entire responsibility for negotiation, a newspaper management would be obliged to communicate to employees its company's objectives (hopefully including an obligation to make a profit), its company's hopes for the future, and most importantly, its personnel and industrial relations policy.

Apart from equally obvious management duties like formalising and publicising its management structure there would seem little more to do than work for success to ensure that the maximum number of titles live on into the foreseeable future. There is no reason why a strategy for the eighties should not begin now.

Some of the general secretaries took the initiative in setting up the talks which created the Joint Standing Committee. It is not too late, not quite too late, for Fleet Street's managements to take the initiative to change the industry's bargaining arrangements.

PART III

Fleet Street

6 The development of market segments: an outline of the factors involved

MICHAEL SHIELDS

Managing Director, Associated Newspapers Group Limited

Michael Shields joined Associated Newspapers in the Advertisement department after University and service in the Royal Artillery during the war. After a period as a representative on the selling side of the various papers in the Group he specialised in the application of readership studies on the selling of space. He then spent several years in various departments of the Group—Circulation, Editorial and Management—and also spent a year on loan at Associated Rediffusion in charge of Audience Research. He returned to Associated Newspapers in charge of a newly-established research department and thereafter set up a research subsidiary, National Opinion Polls.

He is now the Managing Director of Associated Newspapers Group Limited, and holds Directorships in various associated companies. He is a member of the Executive Council of the Advertising Association, a Fellow of the Royal Statistical Society and is also on the council of the Newspaper Publishers Association.

It is proposed to discuss some of the ways in which an existing publishing company can extend its activities profitably. Accordingly, the areas which will be covered include:

(i)   The ways in which ideas arise;
(ii)   the integration of these new ventures within the current structure of the company;
(iii) the financial considerations and decision-making under conditions of uncertainty;
(iv)   the factors to be considered in securing and holding the segment;
(v)   comments on staffing requirements.

The accompanying chart outlines some of the problem areas and also the points which should not be neglected or taken for granted if one wishes to have a successful operation.

An existing publishing company is likely to have resources of printing machinery, printing operatives, sales forces, transport facilities and journalists, together with the management structure of existing publications. Thus, if a publishing company should decide that there is a market segment, it does not necessarily mean that a new and separate publication should be produced to cater for this publishing opportunity. It may, instead, be possible to extend or to modify an existing publication in order to achieve a greater profitability. An analysis of the resources which a company possesses, such as capital, production capacity, sales forces and personnel, may have shown that some of these resources are under-utilised.

A 'market segment', or a market opportunity, can thus be defined in the following ways:

1. The realisation that a group of people exists, with similar

interests or needs, which is not at the moment served by a publication and for whom a new publication can therefore be started. An example, here, is our highly successful international financial magazine *Euromoney.*

2. The realisation that there exists, within the readers of one of our established publications, a need for information on a particular subject and also that there exist advertisers who wish to reach this group. Examples of this, in the industry, are *Money Mail,* published as a supplement on Wednesdays in the *Daily Mail, Education Guardian* in the *Guardian* on Tuesdays, *Europa* published monthly in *The Times,* a recently established Antiques Page published on Mondays in the *Daily Mail* and the reports and supplements on various industries and foreign countries in *The Times* and *The Financial Times.*

3. An opportunity can arise by one perceiving the decline or failure of an existing publication belonging to another company. There are several choices here, including:

   (i) One can purchase the publication, which may still have commendable contents and an adequate circulation but which for reasons of overheads and other costs is not profitable to its present owners. The purchaser, however, may have considerable unused potential in terms of printing and publishing facilities and sales forces. Thus he may well be able to run the magazine on a marginal costing basis, using his present staff.

   (ii) If a publication were to cease, for economic reasons, rather than for reasons of disenchantment amongst current readers, one can either start another publication or one can extend an existing publication to retain as much as possible of the readership and advertisement revenues which have become available.

   (iii) It may become clear and appear highly likely that a

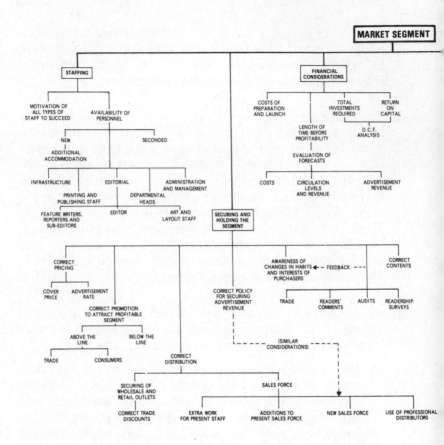

Figure 6.1 The evaluation of a new opportunity within an existing company

radical change in the format of an existing publication will produce extra circulation and advertisement revenue and a higher profitability. This has been demonstrated, in recent years, by the *Daily Mail* and the *Sun*.

It will be seen that, because different types of opportunities exist—which could be looked upon as different ways of

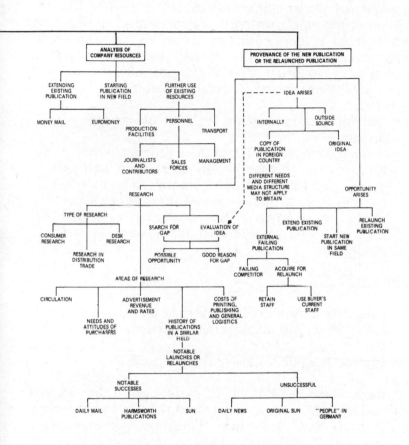

approaching the concept of a 'market segment'—one of the most important tasks in an existing company is to analyse the resources of this company and see how they can be utilised with the minimum extra investment. It is important, though, to have an existing staff which has a high degree of involvement in its work and also good contacts with the printing and distribution trades. Thus, firstly, a flow of ideas will be generated and, secondly, the possible ventures will be filtered into a smaller number of probable opportunities.

Some of the points within the 'Provenance' section have been covered in the definitions above. A very important point, though, is the 'validity' or the 'quality' of the gap, in the first place. As Brian Allt (1974) points out, the sequence of new publishing ventures is, as often as not:

'Producing a publication for a particular type of person.
Hoping there are enough of these people around.
Finding out whether it sells enough to keep it going—and, of course, if it doesn't sell enough, not knowing whether one aimed at the wrong set of people, misunderstood their needs, overestimated their numbers, or produced the wrong kind of publication'

rather than

'Identifying a group of people to be aimed at.
Establishing how many of them there are.
Establishing their needs.
Producing a publication to fit their needs.'

This leads to the question of the evaluation of the risk in a new venture, which comes partly into the 'Research' section of the chart and partly into 'Financial Considerations'. Clearly, one is making a decision under conditions of uncertainty and thus the background research must have been carried out thoroughly and imaginatively. However, the required background in which a decision on a new venture is made is a planned management approach (see Waterworth (1972)), which comprises:

'a) Setting clear objectives.
b) Considering plans and selecting the 'best'.
c) Controlling activities to ensure that the plans are working.'

Thus it is expected that every effort will have been made to quantify the financial proposition which is submitted. It is necessary to have, very clearly spelled out:

(i)   the nature of the publication;
(ii)   the nature and number of the potential purchasers;
(iii)   the likely advertisement revenue;
(iv)   the costs of paper, printing and distribution;
(v)   the costs of personnel, accommodation and other expenses and the availability of the personnel;
(vi)   the costs of promotion;
(vii)   an analysis of other publications in the market and their profitabilities;
(viii) the opinions of the wholesale and retail trade;
(ix)   a detailed statement of cash flow;

in order to see how much money will be needed, for how long, before the venture begins to show a return.

It should be mentioned here that this method is in regular use with our subsidiary, Harmsworth Publications, which sells over two million paperbacks per year, generally with between 50000 and 100000 sales per title and which introduces up to half a dozen new titles per year. (See Heenan and Addleman (1976) and Moore (1977) for discussions of the quantitative approach to preparing financial propositions and making financial decisions.)

A publication which has been started has to succeed and become profitable very much in a nation-wide or fully launched situation, as the high first-copy costs generally mean that a test-market is not possible. Continual effort and encouragement has to be put into the operation and there must be constant attention to detail in many fields of activity to support the editorial format and content. Kobak (1977) in a check-list of 186 points for the attention of the publisher of a new magazine, discusses, in detail, editorial contents, printing, advertisement revenue, circulation and service to consumers and suggests:

> 'Continue to re-sell the investors.
> Continue to re-sell your staff.
> Don't be so excited that you carry on even though the stop signal is there.
> Work an 18-hour day including Sundays and holidays.
> Get your spouse interested and useful in the project.
> It's cheaper and less time-consuming than a divorce.'

... amongst other useful recommendations.

It will have been seen that financial considerations are very important in evaluating new opportunities. Also one has to be sure that any new venture can reasonably fit into the existing organisation, in terms of availability of staff, accommodation and management. Established publishers will find that many ideas are generated internally or are offered from outside, often with glowing recommendations that a particular idea should not be missed. If, though, one is in any doubt about giving the go-ahead on a new venture, the answer is 'Don't'.

It is always warmer in bed!

The author would like to acknowledge Martin MacDonald's great assistance in the writing of this contribution.

References

Allt, Brian, *Research for Editors,* ESOMAR 1974.
Bird, Michael, *Publishers, Editors and Researchers,* ESOMAR 1974.
ESOMAR Papers. General reference can be made to the papers on market segmentation, pricing, promotion and editorial content in: *Marketing and Research in the*

Publishing Industry Munich. 8-11 November 1972, and *Editorial Research in the Publishing Industry* Parts I and II, Verona, 16-19 October 1974.

Hansen, Fleming, *Newspaper Segmentation Based Upon Content and Treatment Factors,* ESOMAR 1974.

Heenan, David A. and Addleman, Robert B., 'Quantitative Techniques for Today's Decision Makers', *Harvard Business Review,* May-June 1976, pp 32-62.

Johnson, Richard M., 'Market Segmentation: A Strategic Management Tool', *Journal of Marketing Research,* Vol. 8 (February 1971), pp 13-18.

Kobak, James B, 'Now That You've Raised the Money for a New Magazine', *Folio Magazine* (New Canaan, Connecticut), February 1977, Vol. 6, No. 2, pp 34-40.

Moore, P.G. 'The Manager's Struggles with Uncertainty', *Journal of the Royal Statistical Society,* Series A, Vol. 140, Part 2, 1977, pp 129-165.

Royal Commission on the Press *Final Report* Cmnd 6810. Appendices Cmnd 6810—1. HMSO July 1977.

Waterworth, Derek, 'The Process of Management', *Marketing Forum,* May-June 1972, pp 9-14.

Wills, Gordon, 'Product Strategy' in: *Creating and Marketing New Products,* University of Bradford Management Centre, February 16-21 1969.

7 The integration of advertising and circulation sales policies

MICHAEL MANDER

Deputy Chief Executive, Times Newspapers Limited

Michael Mander has been in the newspaper industry since 1956, following his education in Britain and the United States and two years National Service. He joined Times Newspapers as Advertisement and Marketing Director in 1971, after fifteen years with Associated Newspapers where he was involved in circulation, production, general management and marketing in Scotland, Manchester and London. He was appointed Deputy Chief Executive and Marketing Director of Times Newspapers in 1977. He is a Council Member of the Institute of Directors, a Fellow of the Institute of Marketing and on the Council of the NPA, Advertising Association and JICNARS.

Most people inside Fleet Street, and some outside, claim a knowledge of the *finances* of the national newspapers industry. That far fewer, even inside, understand the *economics* of the business may begin to explain some of the problems that face many newspapers. Perhaps it is not surprising, given the history of ownership of most of the current titles, that normal business methods and objectives have often been absent from Fleet Street.

It has become usual, not altogether without justification, for managements to blame their predecessors for today's problems. This is usually taken to mean that the previous generation of owners, rich enough to afford it, would pay the necessary price to ensure continuity of production. Hence the strength of unions, and the inherited weakness of today's management's position. While all this may be true, the real inheritance had much deeper faults.

Historically—up to 1939—owners, editors and managers devoted themselves to the pursuit of circulation. Bizarre as the circulation battles may have become, the objective was right. Whatever the motivation may have been, the result for most papers was profit. The costs of paper and production were low enough for cover prices to produce healthy margins. Empires grew, barons prospered—and circulation had become the Holy Grail.

Sales were created by innovative and sensational journalism and excellent distribution backed by inventive promotion. Meanwhile, advertising was of secondary importance, although highly valued. While the power and the profit came from circulation, advertising was a fortuitous bonus. To editors, advertising was a necessary evil—an intrusion into the real purpose of a newspaper. By today's standards, it was bought and sold in an unsophisticated way, based on whim and fancy rather than on statistics—which were few and suspect. The papers that succeeded were those that had the best salesmen. They were not selling their readership, they were selling themselves. (Read Bill Needham's *50 Years of Fleet Street* and see).

So two quite separate characters grew up—Circulation Man, to whom the only measure of success was rising sales, as it was to editors; and Advertising Man, who could sell independently of the size or nature of his paper's circulation.

Years later, after the War and newsprint rationing, the scene had changed. The public were saturated with newspapers; this was no longer a growth market. The massive promotional antics of the thirties no longer produced the same results; fortunes were frittered away. Labour costs grew, and the days of fat profits had gone.

But advertising was becoming big business. After the austerity of the forties, people were demanding a better standard of living, and demanding the money to afford it. As the consumer goods boom gathered momentum, advertising appropriations grew rapidly. And with that growth came the beginnings of media buying based not on handshakes and gin-and-tonics, but on unemotional value-for-money criteria. Advertisers demanded, and media provided, firstly proof of circulation, closely followed by detailed research into readership. Salesmanship was no longer enough by itself.

By the mid-fifties those newspapers that had gathered for themselves—by skill, chance or intuition—readerships that were either very big or small but specialised were the ones that prospered. The rest died. Between 1955 and 1961, no less than six papers closed or merged. They varied in circulation from the *Empire News*—2.1 million—to *Reynolds News* at 300000. But they had one thing in common—no defined and saleable advertisement market (see Figure 7.1). However successful Circulation Man may have been in the past, and however genial, well-connected and generous Advertising Man, their skills had been separate—even divergent. It would have been almost inconceivable then for one of those dead papers' Circulation Man to have reversed the instincts of years, and proposed a *smaller* circulation for his paper and a higher cover price. Even if he could have convinced his board, could he have swayed the editor? The traditions inherited were just too strong.

Even today, in most Fleet Street houses, the separation of circulation and advertising continues—even to board level. Only Times Newspapers, News International and more recently Harmsworth, have created a joint commercial management, where policy seems to be considered as a whole rather than in two parts. Many chief executives will say that they represent the functions of the chief marketing executive, thus ensuring co-ordinated commercial policies, but in practice may have to spend such a large proportion of their time involved in industrial relations that it is virtually impossible to do justice to both functions.

Whatever the structures may be, it is evident that there are still lessons from the past to be learned. A few newspapers are still poised in the middle ground between the mass market and the small specialist readerships.

From 1967 to 1969 *The Times,* under its new ownership by the Thomson Organisation moved into dangerous waters. Its sale shot from 270000 to 450000—a remarkable achievement. But its higher sale made it no more attractive as an advertisement medium. It already had its corner of the market established; adding to the readership just watered down the essential target group, and increased the cost of reaching it. A reversal of policy changed the situation with a consequent dramatic improvement in profitability. The circulation is back down to just under 300000.

The chase for circulation is still very evident among the popular[1] papers. Cover prices are still modest, and almost identical; promotion is still vigorous; and what is assumed to be popular taste is assiduously courted editorially. And it is still the right objective. While the marginal costs of production are less than the net cover price income, every extra copy contributes towards profit.

The circulation policy seems to be to sell enough extra copies to create enough marginal contribution to cover fixed costs—and thus make a real profit. The problem with that is that the market is declining and it is probably an impossible objective for all five of them.

The advertisement policy of the 'populars' is mostly related to being big. But that alone is no guarantee of success. It is a packed advertisement market with not only competition from other populars but also from women's magazines, television

[1] For the purpose of this discussion, the term 'popular' applies only to the *Daily Mirror, Sun, News of the World, Sunday People* and *Sunday Mirror.*

and radio. Advertisement rates, nuances of specialisation and editorial flavour all play their part in sharing out media money. So does selling.

Not all papers are in a run-on profit situation. The quality Sundays, with their magazines, all lose money on the marginal extra copy. Even at a price of 22p, the net circulation income per copy of *The Sunday Times* is lower than the cost of paper, ink and carriage. In the short term, small losses of sale are a positive benefit to profit. Circulation policy for all of the quality press is not to create as big a circulation as possible, but to maintain a sale sufficiently high, and of an appropriate nature, to command a slice of advertisement markets at an acceptable advertisement rate. In reality there is no such thing as a circulation policy—there is just commercial policy.

The new economics of national newspapers have changed dramatically in the last few years in absolute terms, and in the internal balances of costs and revenues.

The biggest impact on costs has been the price of newsprint. It has been forced up by a greater world demand from developing nations; by the price of energy, a lot of which is used in manufacture; and by the devaluation of sterling against Scandinavian and Canadian currencies. In Times Newspapers, newsprint now represents thirty per cent of total costs, against only twenty per cent in 1970.

Revenue sources have changed too. Cover prices, too long held down by competitive fears, are at last becoming more realistic. It is not easy to catch up, and circulations in general have fallen in the face of rapid price increases.

Advertisement rates have been forced up too, yet limited by the wider competition from magazines and television as much as from other newspapers.

The balance between advertisement and circulation income differs from paper to paper. In general, the qualities are moving towards a greater reliance on cover price income, as sales have been more stable than those of the populars, and have withstood higher prices better. Conversely, the populars are moving the other way: cover prices are more sensitive, competition is acute. The *Sun* effectively prevents its competitors from advancing prices very far, despite the big revenue potential. So advertisement revenue is becoming relatively more important, though constrained by the tight competition. Not surprisingly, selling initiative is at a premium.

While the qualities and populars are conducting their separate battles for profit, what of the papers in between, and so much in the news? The *Daily Mail* and *Daily Express* not so long ago found themselves perilously close to a sort of Bermuda Triangle—the graveyard of mastheads that have disappeared under the increased costs and diminished revenues.

Figure 7.1 shows the last reported position of those national newspapers that have sunk since 1955, as well as the current plots of the survivors. The axes are circulation and the ABC1 share of profile. The vulnerability of the *Express* and *Mail* are highlighted; they have been in the past neither big enough to challenge the advertisement markets of the populard, nor specialised enough to challenge the qualities.

The *Mail* however, successfully pulled itself away from the magnet of this triangle by an editorially brilliant relaunch, sophisticated promotion and a single mindedness among editorial and commercial executives about their objectives that came through clearly to readers, agencies and advertisers alike, and at their present rate of progress seem likely to pull themselves further away from the danger area.

The *Daily Express* on the other hand, until the recent take-over, appeared to be floating dangerously towards the ship wreck area. Hopefully for the industry Trafalgar's ownership has given it the opportunity and resources to reverse the trend.

The key question is whether a big enough advertisement market exists, or can be persuaded to exist, to match their circumstances; or whether through editorial change they can alter the nature and size of their readership enough to move into the already strongly competitive markets of the populars or the qualities. No easy task. In a recent announcement the

Express implied that a decision had been made to go down market, and aim for a three million circulation. In as much as the *Mail* has moved into the upper side of the middle market, there would on the surface seem to be some logic in the *Express* cornering for itself the lower side of the middle market, and if this is their objective everyone (not least the *Mail*) will wish them well. But if ever there was a case for a strong co-ordinated commercial/marketing policy, undistracted by the equally critical but onerous burden of dealing with industrial relations as well, it is surely going to be needed in the next stage of the development of the *Express*.

In the case of Fleet Street titles now, more than ever before, it is time for Advertising Man and Circulation Man, not to mention owners and editors, to hammer out a single commercial policy. The reversal, or abandonment of tradition and instinct can be a painful process—for some, higher cover prices and smaller sales; for others, the abandonment of some of their traditional readers if that is what they decide to do.

Of course, in the case of both the *Mail* and the *Express* their economics are going to be vitally affected by the effect on the cost of their overheads of any developments in the London evening paper situation. This does not, however, in any way water down the vital need for a co-ordinated incisive commercial/marketing strategy to secure their own—or any Fleet Street newspaper's—further prosperity.

No review of the economics of Fleet Street would be complete without reference to the much discussed new technology. I have left it until last because when it happens, which it assuredly will, it would be exceptionally dangerous for it to be regarded, particularly within Fleet Street, as a panacea. That some companies will not have a long-term future without it is certain. However, at worst it will cut costs once, buy time for those papers that need it, and give needed strength to compete with other media. It can prevent immediate disasters, but like North Sea oil its year by year benefits will diminish. Only editorial skills and innovation with the support and within the framework of a co-ordinated

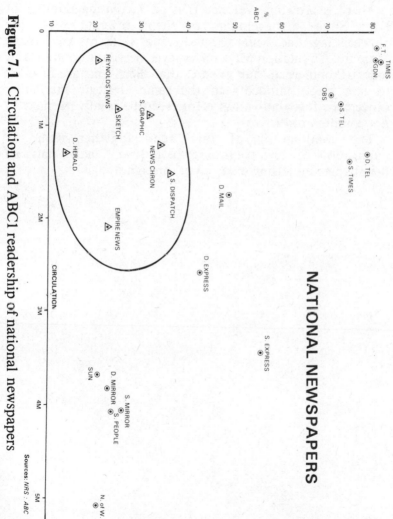

Figure 7.1 Circulation and ABC1 readership of national newspapers

Sources: *NRS* : *ABC*

commercial policy can secure the long-term prosperity of individual titles.

There is growing evidence that an increasing number of Fleet Street managements in their different ways are appreciating that, while the individual skills of Advertising Man and Circulation Man have never been more important, unless Commercial Man ensures that their skills are blended to aim single mindedly at the same strategic marketing objectives, their individual efforts can be totally masked, if not counter productive.

The combination of this trend together with the application of new technology could well make national newspapers the strong medium of the eighties.

8 How to change direction without losing what you already have

BRIAN NICHOLSON

Joint Managing Director, The Observer

Brian Nicholson started his career as a journalist on the Newcastle Journal and Evening Chronicle, and after a year in Canada working as a reporter and an advertisement salesman, rejoined Kemsley Newspapers (subsequently Thomson) as Classified Manager, first in Manchester and then in Cardiff. He transferred to The Sunday Times in 1956, and rose through the advertising hierarchy to become an executive director of that newspaper in 1963. In 1965 he changed to Beaverbrook Newspapers becoming Joint Deputy Managing Director in 1976. He joined The Observer in May 1977.

The national newspaper industry traditionally fails to learn from its mistakes. That awful expression 'relaunch' has been used far too often by newspaper managements as a crazy kind

of panacea full of hope that this time perhaps a new editor
and lots of money for promotion will start to make
circulation rise, that advertisers' confidence will be restored
and the newspaper will be returned to profit.

What managements and editors constantly forget is that
their regular readers (and most of them *are* regular) have got
accustomed to their paper as it is. They may well have read it
from childhood. It is almost part of the furniture, and over
the years they have liked it as it is and probably have not
noticed gradual changes in content and format. But a major
change in the paper may be the factor leading them to decide
to try another in its place.

The Observer currently presents a fascinating challenge to
its editor and its management. On the surface, it has the
traditional problems of falling sales and readership. Today
the sale is 656242 (ABC, Jan-June 1977), over 250000 down
on its peak in 1967, and readership has also evidenced a fall
to a figure now of 2092000 (July 1976-June 1977).

It would be easy to be depressed by this state of affairs and
to start looking for drastic remedies to try and restore the
paper to its former position and strength. But I am very much
against trying to make dramatic changes to the editorial style
of the newspaper, in the expectation that existing readers will
accept them and new readers come along in droves.

In my judgement, *The Observer* must be viewed in the
context of an extremely strong and highly significant
market—that of quality Sunday newspapers as a whole.
Between 1946 and 1976, though the circulation of the popular
Sundays fell by over thirty per cent, the sales of quality
Sundays rose from approximately 877000 to no less than
2811000. Admittedly *The Sunday Times* enjoys a sale almost
double that of *The Observer,* while the *Sunday Telegraph,*
with the relatively recent transference of the colour
supplement to Sunday publication, has now increased its
circulation to 800000 easily overtaking *The Observer* as it
does so.

A management could be forgiven for being discouraged by
such a state of affairs. However, it must be recognised that

The Observer has a hard core of loyal readers whose needs cannot be ignored. Their existence is confirmation of the vital role *The Observer* performs in the total quality Sunday market. The solution is to build on this foundation, using it as a firm base for improving sales and readership.

The tough times *The Observer* has experienced in recent years has prevented money being spent either on investment in new features in the paper or to promote itself in competition with the other Sunday newspapers. Its acquisition in early 1977 by Atlantic Richfield, an American oil company, has given its management the opportunity both to promote the newspaper and to improve it as a product through increases in the editorial budget.

One of the major decisions taken in 1977 was to increase the price of the newspaper at the beginning of June by twenty per cent—from 15p to 18p. This put *The Observer* 4p more than the *Sunday Telegraph* and closer to *The Sunday Times* at 22p. The decision was taken not so much to bring in much needed additional revenue as to position the newspaper in its correct place in the market.

Certainly the *Sunday Telegraph* must have a considerable volume advantage in selling at a price so much less than the other two quality Sundays. But its price is unrealistic in relation to what the public will pay for quality weekly newspapers. Similarly, of course, the *Daily Telegraph* at 9p is ridiculously under-priced in relation to *The Times* and the *Guardian*.

However, the effect of the price increase of *The Observer* was not, as might have been expected, to bring the sales down. Instead, aided by some vigorous promotion of editorial features (mainly on television), sales increased for the three month period that followed the date of the increase. September sales could average around 700000.

I am sure that the fact that there are three newspapers in the Sunday quality market makes it a significantly stronger market than if there were two. This sounds palpably obvious, but Fleet Street managements have usually measured their success by their ability to grind their competitors into the

dust. The argument has often been heard that if there were
only one London evening newspaper, then that newspaper
would make huge profits—instead of both the present
evenings losing at a rate estimated recently of over £5 million
a year. The argument falls down in my view because
advertisers need choice and coverage, and one single evening
newspaper would not sell the same number of copies as the
present two evenings combined. Where the sale of the two
London evenings todlay totals to just under one million, a
monopoly evening would sell only between 700000-800000.
Much the same argument must apply to the Sundays, and I
believe that this market with a total sale of 18 849 149 (all) and
2 826 183 (quality), and total readership of 34 099 000 (all) and
8 129 000 (quality) represents a force that must be respected by
advertisers and advertising agencies, so that any change of
direction that *The Observer* takes has to be done discreetly
and subtly.

The tastes and habits of existing readers must be respected,
and the process of attracting new readers should be seen in
terms of not just one massive promotion campaign, but of a
programme encompassing all aspects of the newspaper and
carrying on indefinitely. Hopefully, existing readers like the
new things they see in the newspaper and casual readers are
converted into regular readers.

One thing not to do is to try and make the newspaper
cheaper or to go down market. The research that *The
Observer* has carried out over the years, and especially
recently, indicates very clearly the possessive nature of the
average reader's attitude to the paper: I do not suppose this
differs in any way from similar research commissioned by
other newspapers in the same field. Not unexpectedly, there is
a considerable loyalty to established writers—in the case of
The Observer, particularly to such writers as Katherine
Whitehorn and Clive James.

In a recent group interview, one of the people present said,
'I always get *The Observer.* It's familiarity, it's not the
headline itself or the layout, or type, or whatever—it's the
recognition of the paper you know and you like.' Other

people stress that their allegiance to *The Observer* is because it is a radical paper, not as conservative as *The Times* or *Telegraph.*

What is clear is that the readers of *The Observer* have a commitment to the newspaper which represents a vital part of the way they spend their leisure.

What they need in my view is to be reassured that their newspaper will give them everything they can get from another newspaper, plus a bit more. They key to this must be first of all, of course, the best possible editorial mix, and secondly really effective promotion of the newspaper. This will ensure that regular readers and casual readers are aware of what is happening in the newspaper; of the features that are appearing or are to appear; of the exclusives that are the life blood of a good newspaper. Nothing reassures a reader more than to feel that his or her newspaper is close to what is going on in the country. *The Observer* has had its fair share of such exclusives already in 1977.

9 You buy — we sell

TONY BASSETT-POWELL

Advertisement Director, The Daily Telegraph

In the period from 1 January 1970 to 31 December 1976 the average circulations of all national dailies fluctuated considerably. The demise of the *Sketch,* the change in format of the *Daily Mail* in May 1971 and the phenomenal growth of the *Sun* were the contributory factors.

The switch to decimalisation in February 1971 and subsequent price increases together with the factors mentioned above resulted in a sharp falling off in sales that year, but a steady recovery commenced, until in 1974 they had passed the level of 1970, and showed every indication of progressing further.

By the end of 1974 however, the sudden rise in newsprint prices allied with other increasing costs, and the rapidly diminishing revenue from display advertising forced the press in general to increase cover prices to a level for which the consumer was unprepared. As a result 1975 saw a drop in circulation which has continued.

In this period the circulation of all quality dailies exceeded 15 per cent of the total market, but their loss in recent years has been proportionately greater than that of the populars. (See Table 9.1a).

By contrast the decline in circulation of national Sundays

a

	1970	1971	1972	1973	1974	1975	1976
Daily newspapers copies sold '000	14,694	14,176	14,324	14,584	14,797	14,112	14,002
Index 1970	100	96.5	97.5	99.3	100.7	96.0	95.3
Popular dailies share %	84.5	84.1	83.9	84.2	84.4	84.8	85.0
Quality dailies share %	15.5	15.9	16.1	15.8	15.6	15.2	15.0

Source: ABC

b

	1970	1971	1972	1973	1974	1975	1976
Sunday newspapers copies sold '000	23,491	22,744	22,091	22,095	21,876	20,495	19,594
Index 1970	100	96.8	94.0	94.1	93.1	87.2	83.4
Popular Sundays' share %	87.1	86.9	86.3	86.0	86.0	86.0	85.7
Quality Sundays' share %	12.9	13.1	13.7	14.0	14.0	14.0	14.3

Source: ABC

Table 9.1 Average issue circulation and share of popular and quality newspapers

has been continuously steady, the qualities marginally but progressively increasing their share in this period. (Table 9.1b).

It might be reasonable to suppose that purchasers of newspapers are least willing to forgo their daily paper, and will sacrifice their Sunday paper (especially where they are buyers of primary and secondary publications) when the costs seem exorbitant. We know that magazines, particularly programme journals, are the most vulnerable in these circumstances.

While increasing costs have resulted in diminishing circulation, falling circulation has inevitably meant rising costs, and Tables 9.2a and 9.2b illustrate the trend over the period under review.

The national dailies cost 152 per cent more in 1976 than they did in 1970, while selling 4.7 per cent fewer copies; the Sundays 130 per cent more despite a circulation loss of 16.6 per cent.

The quality dailies' share of the total spent rose sharply to its peak in 1972 and has gradually levelled to 20+ per cent. The quality Sundays' share peaked in 1975 after a gradual increase since 1970. Their drop in 1976 reflects their fall in circulation, which is not yet compensated by their cover price increases.

Although the quality press lost circulation in the period 1970 to 1976 it marginally increased its ABC1 readership, consolidating a demographic profile least vulnerable to threat by TV, and rich in potential for both display and classified advertising.

In the period reviewed here the qualities increased their display advertisement revenue by 108 per cent (at card rates) compared with the increase of 96 per cent obtained by the press as a whole. (See Table 9.3a).

While 1973-4 was a difficult period for display advertising, it produced an abundancy of classified in the quality press, exceeding even the high levels obtained in 1970. (See Table 9.3b). It should be noted that while the dailies are 14 per cent down in terms of columnage and the Sundays 0.5 per cent

a

	1970	1971	1972	1973	1974	1975	1976
On daily newspapers £'000	109,701	128,437	140,651	145,106	195,390	246,165	276,758
Index 1970 = 100	100	117	128	132	178	224	252
Popular dailies share %	82.1	78.7	77.8	78.3	79.6	79.1	79.3
Quality dailies share %	17.9	21.3	22.2	21.7	20.4	20.9	20.7

Source: ABC and Telegraph Marketing

b

	1970	1971	1972	1973	1974	1975	1976
On Sunday newspapers £'000	45,599	51,462	61,472	62,644	72,900	76,656	104,959
Index 1970 = 100	100	113	135	137	160	168	230
Popular Sundays' share %	81.6	81.7	81.9	79.8	79.1	75.3	78.9
Quality Sundays' share %	18.4	18.3	18.1	20.2	20.9	24.7	21.1

Source: ABC and Telegraph Marketing

Table 9.2 Total consumers' expenditure and share of popular and quality national newspapers

The Daily Telegraph Limited Year to 31.3.77	Net receipts %
Income from sales	43.27
Income from advertising	56.24
Miscellaneous revenue	.42
Paid-for publications	.07
	100.00

	Expenditure %
Salaries, wages, National Insurance	33.48
*Paper and ink	36.13
Distribution including road and rail carriage	6.64
News service and reporting expenses	5.01
Production costs (excluding paper and ink)	1.40
General establishment charges	5.54
Contract printing	8.34
Depreciation	.68
Promotion and publicity	1.68
Profit (subject to tax)	1.10
	100.00

*Costs of paper and ink have increased by 280% since 1970.

Figure 9.1

below the 1970 level, rates have increased by approximately 63 per cent and 69 per cent, respectively, between these years.

Statistically, the qualities appear to be over the hump, and the first six months of 1977 are even more encouraging. Or are they?

Without the introduction of new printing technology, discussed elsewhere in this book, together with a streamlining of the work force, the survival of the quality press as we know it today must be in serious doubt.

a

Indices of Display Advertisement Expenditure, 1970-1976

	1970 '000	1970	1971	1972	1973	1974	1975	1976
TV (MEAL)	£144,116	100	115	145	156	155	197	247
MEAL selected press	£168,054	100	109	130	144	146	163	196
Total of above	£312,170	100	112	137	150	150	189	219
Quality dailies	£17,735	100	115	149	163	159	167	210
Quality Sundays	£7,176	100	119	160	152	146	166	198
*All qualities total	£24,911	100	116	152	160	155	167	208
Retail Price Index		100	109	117	128	148	185	215

*Weekend magazines are not included.

Source: MEAL

b

Indices of Classified Advertising Volumes

	1970 Columns	1970	1971	1972	1973	1974	1975	1976
Quality dailies	45,618	100	84.4	99.5	130.3	119.3	90.5	86.0
Quality Sundays	15,467	100	84.7	100.6	116.4	121.1	92.2	99.5
All qualities total	61,085	100	84.5	99.8	126.8	119.8	90.9	89.4

Source: *The Daily Telegraph Market Research*

Table 9.3 Indices of advertising expenditure and volumes

The Daily Telegraph Limited, perhaps one of the more 'prosperous' of the group, showed a net profit, subject to tax, of 1.10 per cent of the turnover in the financial year ending 31 March 1977. Hardly sufficient to encourage investment!

Theirs is an interesting balance sheet (see Figure 9.1), and in profile terms maybe the other publishers of quality newspapers are in a similar position.

It does not require a David Attenborough to explain that like will turn on like if a species is threatened by a shrinking supply of whatever is essential to its survival, and competition for circulation and advertising has always been fierce among the publications which comprise the quality press.

What is unusual, if not unique, is the united effort these publications have made to challenge the necessity for the shrinkage.

The Business Media Research Committee, or now 'New Business Research Consortium' represents such a combined effort, and since its first Businessman Research Survey in 1973 has considerably expanded a market which had previously been static.

Of equal importance, this joint research has qualified as well as quantified the behavioural characteristics of each publication across the many and diverse classifications within the businessman market. In so doing it demonstrated the difference between the newspapers which comprise the quality press and emphasised the inter-dependence of each in providing an effective media group.

10 A market in search of a newspaper?

PETER A. CLARK

Secretary-General, Market Research Society

Peter Clark is Secretary-General of the Market Research Society, which he joined in 1977 from the Evening Newspaper Advertising Bureau. He joined ENAB on its formation in 1962 and as the Bureau's head of research and information, has become an acknowledged authority on the regional press. He has served on a number of industry committees dealing with both readership and circulation. Recently he gave evidence and provided statistical information for the Royal Commission on the Press.

In the first half of 1977 the two London evening newspapers were selling jointly fewer copies than the *Evening News* alone did in 1971. For a decade from the death of the *Star* in 1960, this decline was shared equally in the ratio 65 : 35 *Evening News* : *Evening Standard*. The early seventies saw a change in the pattern as the *Evening Standard* lost sales less rapidly but the *Evening News* still retained over sixty per cent of the London market until the second half of 1974.

A price increase from 3p to 4p for both newspapers in March 1974 halted the *Evening Standard's* upward progress and had a more serious effect on the monthly sales figures of the *Evening News* which dropped by an average seven per cent over each of the succeeding six months. Worse was to come for this newspaper with its change to tabloid format in September 1974. In each of the next nineteen months its sales losses were in double figures and price increases, for both newspapers, in January and again in April 1975 compounded the situation and brought also the *Evening Standard* into the same category of sales loss.

It is not altogether fanciful to suggest that if the *Evening News* had not chosen that point in time to change from broadsheet to tabloid format it would have been in a stronger position to challenge its rival earlier in 1977.

This harsh financial consideration is given a certain piquancy by an incident recounted in A.J.P. Taylor's book *Beaverbrook*. He writes, 'Later in 1931 he (Beaverbrook) suggested moving the *Standard* to the new *Express* building and transforming it to the size of Rothermere's *Evening News*. Rothermere advised against both, particularly the second: it would be a great shock to advertisers and would cost £400 000.'

Changes of format or manning levels or editor will be of no avail until the product is right.

A local paper

In the inability to recognise that a London evening newspaper is a local evening newspaper and not a quasi-national lies the cause of the *News'* and *Standard's* present straits. The printing of a newspaper in London does not confer on it national status nor is there any need to seek that when there is available a market of 7½ million people. Yet, in Greater London, the adult readership has moved downwards in this way over the past four years:

1973	Evening News	31%
	Evening Standard	19%
1974	Evening News	30%
	Evening Standard	19%
1975	Evening News	22%
	Evening Standard	18%
1976	Evening News	24%
	Evening Standard	17%

Source: *NRS*

Many reasons have been advanced for this drop and their general circulation decline—a dwindling population in Central London; more commuters using cars; News at Ten; cover price increases; over-manning and union intractability. All contributory factors but perhaps a more cogent reason is the newspapers' basic lack of appeal to those who inhabit, work in and visit London.

Contrast these readership levels, in Greater London, with the seventy per cent household coverage that regional evenings obtain in their towns of publication. While it is true that London evenings are members of the NPA (Newspapers Publishers Association) and not the Newspaper Society—though they were members of the latter body from 1889-1916—it is equally true that they are, or should regard themselves as, local newspapers with a local's need for a sound geographical base. The weakness of this has been underlined in recent years as a result of twin pressures of rising distribution costs and competition from the seven evening newspapers which have been founded in the past twelve years on the periphery of London. Yet there are still sales points as far apart as Brighton, Maidstone and Cambridge.

Competition

Given the long-term joint circulation loss, an outsider can view only with bemusement the short-term internecine advertisements that are run by both newspaper. First, these have no apparent effect in switching readers, both newspapers are declining at a similar rate. Second, this bad tempered advertising can be of little encouragement to readers or advertisers. Third, negative advertising—our sales have dropped less than his—must be morale-sapping for each newspapers' employees. Fourth, and most important, the competition of each London evening newspaper is not the presence of the other London evening newspaper. It is the fact that neither newspaper is appealing enough to retain its readers, let alone attract new ones.

That some of Trafalgar's £10 million, and some of the Argyll oil field's proceeds will be used in promotional battles and efforts to drive the other paper off the streets seems inevitable. But, to repeat, the other newspaper is not the enemy: customer apathy is. A more positive use to which the money could be put would be a joint campaign to promote the concept of reading a London evening newspaper. If the total market were expanded each newspaper would stand a chance of sharing the gains: in the currently declining market both newspapers are merely dividing the losses.

The intense personal rivalry since 1933 between the top managements may have engaged their attention to the exclusion of this broader perspective but outside events have proved to be of greater importance than a compulsion to race one's rival to the news stand.

There may be scope to share distribution facilities and, indeed, to agree to prune the less profitable editions.

Local appeal

Earlier this year headlines in the London evenings read 'Concorde gets the All Clear'. That is a suitable headline for a national newspaper but it could have been personalised to '˜Londoners now only 4½ hours from US'. That gives the news some point in the market to which the papers should be addressing themselves. But the market need not only be native Londoners; the country had 9.4 million foreign visitors last year, the majority of whom spent time in the capital. A page of information for foreign visitors, even perhaps in foreign languages, would heighten the relevance of the two papers to this very substantial market. If only one per cent or 94000 visitors bought an evening newspaper that would represent ten per cent of the combined circulation of the *Evening News* and *Evening Standard.*

The London evenings could include such information as theatres listed by type of play, not theatre; location of the different denominations' places of worship: embassy addresses; all night chemists; times of last trains and phone numbers of cab services; restaurants by type of food or price booklet; next day's events of interest.

This type of service may not be considered journalism by the Editor but it might make marketing sense and it might, in the long run, be more satisfying to run that sort of service in a healthy newspaper than to write a column for a dying one. An examination of the London evenings reveals that a substantial proportion of the stories are about London but this only becomes apparent in the copy; the headlines identify the subject matter at the expense of the location of the event.

The London-ness of the evenings is their strength; to deny it is to invite continuing losses of at least this year's magnitude.

A programme that included thinking local, writing for Londoners, strengthening central sales, and co-operating would represent a radical change of attitude. However, the swingeing losses that are being suffered and the change of management at the *Evening Standard* suggest that now is the time to bury old scores, concentrate on the future and aim to give both readers and advertisers the choice of two healthy London evening newspapers.

PART IV

Regional newspapers

11 Cover prices and advertisement rates: how are they determined?

ROGER NICHOLSON

Roger Nicholson is an economist and a former financial journalist. ·He is now Assistant Managing Director of Aberdeen Journals Limited.

Academic economists have a trick which helps explain the mutual animosity that characterises relationships between some business contemporaries and themselves. The academics define certain pre-conditions at the beginning of a think piece. This precautionary warning is followed by the construction of an often elegant, logical, theoretical model from which reasonable conclusions are drawn.

Unless something has gone seriously wrong in the construction of the model once the conditions were laid down, which is not usually the case, the conclusions are wholly valid—within the framework of the original qualifications. The question is how far they are valid in what short-fuse businessmen call the real world.

Understandably, the academics tend to minimise the difference which the construction of the model in hot-house conditions makes to the validity and practical relevance of the conclusions. But businessmen may dismiss the whole exercise as bloody nonsense because of the unreal premises on which it was based.

Trying to write about the forces which help determine cover prices and advertising rates in present circumstances is a bit like getting trapped between the academics and the businessmen. There is one set of considerations which ought to apply. But there is another which is more likely to be predominant at the point where decisions have to be taken.

The academic may say that in that indeterminate but very handy time scale, the long run, inexorable market forces—both costs and revenue—will prevail. There is something in this. But not too much. Short- and long-run considerations do not always work in parallel, and often they are opposed. The twists and turns of the strategy behind the *Daily Express* in the past three years, since the Glasgow production was transferred to Manchester and the DX80 campaign launched, illustrate this point poignantly but not uniquely. *The Times* also re-sculpted its strategy — successfully in terms of readership profile — after striking out in a different direction in the first post-Thomson years when it held a licence to spend money.

Market positioning, the size and scope of the readership profile which is being aimed for, the desired balance between newspaper sales and advertising revenue, the balance within advertising between the revenue from display and classified, and within classified between classified display, semi-display, and linage, elasticity of demand for papers and for advertising at any given time—these are all obviously factors which bear on cover prices and advertising rates, their absolute levels and their relationship to each other, and most newspaper managements have on their files some kind of strategy which spells out the marketing package which they are working towards. But the position is a bit like Ian Smith's attitude towards majority rule. We are marching to a horizon which for a variety of reasons may never be reached.

General market conditions change, and so do management requirements. Thus a sudden jump in the price of newsprint, the collapse of the situations vacant market, even the timetable for submission to the Price Commission, or an interruption to production can all have more to do with price movements at times than the requirements of the previous market strategy.

That said, it is possible to put down some guidelines which most managements will attempt to operate within even when exigency rather than principle is the main reason for price movements.

The most important asset any publication has is the size and shape of its readership profile and its relationship to the market which it has defined for itself.

For totally obvious reasons the daily and weekly newspapers aiming at an integrated quality market for readers and advertisers are both able and obliged to ask at the present time about double the cover price of the mass market nationals or the regionals whose prosperity depends on sustaining a broad-band appeal in their defined geographical markets.

Also obviously, rises in cover prices tend to depress sales. But against the background of the frequency and percentage of price increases which have taken place since decimalisation in February 1971, across the board the demand for newspapers has held up remarkably well, and there is a lot of evidence around to show that market strategy can offset the danger of cover price increases slashing sales.

The Sunday Times has been outstandingly successful over the years in building up and sustaining general interest in its contents among a coalition of ABCs and young readers, and then in creating an additional surge of interest in a special feature, usually a book serialisation ahead of and through a cover price increase.

Features of this sort are invaluable, because they lend themselves to multi-media promotion over a period, which is cost effective, and because they also lend themselves to flashing a message about the sort of paper the publication is trying to be.

The message can be a two-edged weapon, of course. It has worked for *The Sunday Times* with Alanbrooke and Montgomery and Kennedy and Wilson and Crossman. It has not worked for the *Express* with its pursuit of Eichmann, or Ronald Biggs.

Regional papers cannot afford this sort of editorial-orientated campaign, nor the promotional programme to go with it. But there is usually some topical or regional peg around which a promotional campaign can be built. A few years ago the *Western Mail* went through its most successful cover price increase on a rising sales trend because it built its promotional campaign around the visit of the All Blacks to South Wales, and *The Scotsman* in Edinburgh has just gone through a twenty-five per cent increase with hardly a tremor on an editorial and promotional campaign related to the Scottish debate on the economics of self-government.

Cover prices lead a double life. They bring in revenue. They help define the size and scope of the readership. In turn, therefore, they also have a bearing on the structure of advertising rates. But the only direct link between cover prices and advertising rates is established when management is taking a view of the desired mix between newspaper sales and advertising revenue.

Again for obvious reasons, this varies enormously from one end of the market to the other. At the top end, a paper like *The Financial Times* gets most of its direct revenue from advertising. Likewise, the *Mirror* and the *Sun* get a higher proportion from newspaper sales. In the regional press the proportion used to be about 50 : 50 but probably the balance has tilted towards advertising revenue in the past few years. The 50 : 50 situation is probably ideal, but its attractions can be exaggerated. The important thing is to maintain the readership size and shape of the defined market.

The strictures which were mentioned at the beginning of this article about how the revenue mix is determined in practice apply perhaps with greater force to the level and spread of advertising rates at any given time.

The longer range objectives are usually clear. But more subjective considerations may influence what goes on the rate card, and the rate card may not always reflect what is really happening, depending on market circumstances, the nerve of the advertisement director, and so on.

The story is told of the Irish media buyer who was so thick he paid full rate for a page in a special feature in the *Guardian/Daily Express/Europa*—the publication changes depending on who is telling the story, although the Irish person remains a constant—appearing on August Bank Holiday Monday.

But again there are some guidelines. Obviously, there is a strong relationship between the size and shape of the readership profile and the advertising rates for ROP display per 1000 readers. If these were the only considerations, however, a lot of people, not just Irish media buyers, would be out of work.

The challenge is to define not just a constituency but the special flavour of that constituency and its individual moving parts. The moving parts are fairly easy to define—the number of readers or businessmen of whoever within the framework of the JICNARS (Joint Industry Committee for National Readership Survey) socio-economic categories. The flavour is more difficult. There ought to be a difference between say *The Sunday Times'* ABs and the *Daily Telegraph's* ABs where they are not actually the same people. But what are those differences, and what do they mean to advertisers?

Regional evening papers have a different kind of problem in trying to broaden media buyers' perspective. By and large they are two to three times more expensive per 1000 readers against the popular dailies. But they often deliver over seventy per cent household penetration in retail heartlands, and at their best they have a valuable though difficult task to quantify connection with the communities which they serve.

In discussing advertising rates, attention tends to be focused on display, largely because that is the category with which the big agencies are most involved. But classified is more important to many newspapers, because much of it is exclusive to newspapers, because over the past fifteen years or so it has been, taking one year with another, a growth area, and certainly in the case of the regionals because it is a much more important source of revenue than display.

Classified accounts for about two-thirds of total advertising revenue on most regional papers. In rate card terms, classified is usually more expensive than display, and usually that is the way things turn out on the basis of net column yield. But within the classified columns are probably some items—single insertion BMDs, (Births, Marriages and Deaths) for instance, which do not cover standard costs.

So much, in very general terms, for the present position. For the future, as always, a lot depends on forces outside the control of the industry. But within it I would guess it will get more professional at measuring the value of specific sectors of the market, and of specific positions in the paper, and more professional at measuring the marginal costs of producing different kinds of advertising in different circumstances.

12 *How marketing came to the regional press and what it did for it*

PETER CREED

*Group Advertisement Director, the Express & Star
(Wolverhampton)*

To be precise, it came in 1690, thus:

● **Births**

WORCESTER POST-MAN
(subsequently Berrow's Worcester
Journal). — The first ever newspaper in
the world marketing news and eventually
advertisements. Successful and imitated
elsewhere.

Having quickly answered the question posed by the publisher
as the subject for an article it can be seen that regionals, (you
know, those zombies—north of Watford and generally south
of Wimbledon Common), believe we initiated the industry,
and, what is vitally important, still continue to lead the way.

Had not the publisher himself recently visited England's
first facsimile transmission printing plant at Sandwell *Express
& Star,* one would be tempted to feel here was a cockney in an
ivory tower lazily handing out a publicity crumb for those
amateurs in the sticks, suggesting regionals are dragging
themselves into the seventies with the oh, so sophisticated
national media marketing way-ahead into the eighties.

Then the penny dropped in the thousandth centimetre
particle of my brain. He was needling us to take part and
rightly gauged our reaction. Having bitten the challenge the
flood gates opened, and I was on for 2000 words for nix, of
course, but as a friendly gesture the title could be changed to
suit within decent acceptable reason. Oh no! I always fancied
doing a 'send-up' when given a two minutes impromptu at
public speaking associations on the unreality of people
making speeches just for the sake of it. Now at last I could
have a go at marketing. A nauseating sophisticated word is
marketing!

I never forgave a London newspaper guy acting for a
consortium, which we had paid good money to be a member,
who said our dear *Shropshire Star* (Britain's first web offset
daily—120 miles north of Bow bells) could not have a full
colour Booth's Gin campaign because of 'marketing reasons'
which was supposed to be a final stopper: Mr. Alan Maguire
— advertising manager for Booth's Gin — and Tommy
Rushton of Dorland Advertising accepted the merits and
altered the schedule in favour of the suggestion. So let's settle
for selling—or if it must be all-embracing, merchandising.

A regional newspaper is a family package invited into the
home and it stays there to be handled respectfully by all
members of the family, but of great importance to the
housewife.

The regionals contain a balanced diet of localised news,
views and advertising opportunities. Did not the Evening
Newspaper Advertising Bureau (ENAB) coin a phrase 'all
sales are local'? Look at any regional weekly or evening and
count the thousands of advertisements in the ciassified
columns. Not just situations vacant, but vibrant lines of

opportunities and personal messages which involve readers. The affinity a regional earns with its customers is beyond measurement in cost per thousand, but suffice it to muse that the majority of its readers started in the births columns—graduated to the coming of age column, told friend of their engagement and marriage, found their job, car and house, gained sympathy during bereavements, probably solved family crises in the lost and found columns. Only a regional ad person knows the real joy of linking a pet owner family with another kind reader who had found the stray and through the newspaper is able to get in touch with the other.

Regionals made a significant move forward in the selling of classifieds by importing into this country American methods of telephone canvassing and reception. A pioneer of this in the early fifties was Leslie Stallard of the *Express & Star,* who raised eyebrows by installing a telephone sales department, but it quickly inspired others to follow. Classifieds in the regionals 'took off' to become the major revenue source.

Traders and the general public took advantage of the ease in placing classified advertisements by telephone, and it brought about new sales techniques for improving wording and presentation of advertising through direct speaking contact. National newspapers, food manufacturers and other industries saw the value and developed their own telephone sales departments, modelled on the initiative of Leslie Stallard. He also gave the advertising industry the first and only in-depth survey into the readership of classifieds. Entitled *Out of Darkness...* it was conducted in 1958 and is still well worth quoting in detail:

> 'In common with every other local newspaper, the *Express and Star* has always asserted the affinity that exists between the newspaper and its readers. Without proof of that affinity, however, there has rightly been a shadow of doubt over the real value of the local newspaper to the community it serves. It is this shadow which the *Express and Star* survey has now lifted, and out of

the darkness is revealed the true purpose, and power, of the local press. Here, for the first time in this country or abroad, is unassailable proof of the value of the local newspaper in the advertising pattern. In the results of the survey on the following pages, some assumptions or assertions of the past are confirmed to be solid statements of fact. In many other cases, traditional prejudices have been swept away.

'If up to now, you have been conscious of the shadows, we sincerely believe that this booklet will help you to see the local newspaper in its true light.

'This survey was sponsored by the *Express and Star* and carried out from 29 September to 15 November 1958, by the Research Section of the Newspaper Society. Newspaper Society.

'It concerns, in the main, the readership of classified or (the term preferred by the *Express and Star*) 'Want-Ad' columns. The main objects of the survey were as follows:

a)   To obtain information about 'Want-Ads' which assist the *Express and Star* in giving a better and more comprehensive service to existing and potential advertisers.
b)   To produce a reasoned and factual background of 'Want-Ad' readership as proof of the vital part that local newspapers play in the life of the community.

'That the survey has succeeded in its aims, there is no doubt. The following pages clearly show the influence exerted by the newspaper on the daily lives of the readers. They show the effects on basic needs and predominant interests.

'Houses, jobs, cars and holidays, the modern fundamentals of life, are outstanding in the survey. Surrounding them, the lesser but nevertheless important activities which form the pattern of daily affairs are shown to be materially affected.

'That the newspaper can exert this influence in only

one section of its pages, is surely proof in itself that the newspaper as a whole has a tremendously strong affiliation with the reader—and that its editorial and display columns enjoy the same deep and prolonged readership.

'Here are extracts from the tables which prove the affiliation between the newspaper and its readers:

1) Sixty-nine per cent of our readers look at at least one classification of 'Want-Ads' every evening. Fifty-nine per cent read all the advertisements under that heading.

2) Nearly fifty per cent of the readers who changed their jobs in 1958 did so through the *Express and Star.*

3) About 27000 (ten per cent) men readers changed their jobs during 1958. Of these about thirty-three per cent obtained their job through a 'Want-Ad'.

4) Forty-five per cent of all our readers look at the 'Miscellaneous Sales' column every evening.

5) Over thirty-three per cent of our readers have at some time satisfied their needs as a result of 'Want-Ads'.

6) Over twenty-five per cent of all adults in our area of circulation have done the same thing.

More extracts which prove the results of that affiliation —and thereby the readership which was their source:

1) Over twenty-five per cent of our readers have placed 'Want-Ads' in the *Express and Star.* Seventy per cent of these obtained the results they required.

2) Over twenty-five per cent of the entire adult population within our area of circulation have replied to 'Want-Ads'. Sixty-five per cent of these have been satisfied with the results.

3) One way or the other, thirty-four per cent of all our readers have received satisfactory results from

'Want-Ads'.

4) At least twenty-five per cent of all car sales in the *'Express and Star'* area were made directly as a result of a newspaper advertisement.

5) Fifty-three per cent of all publicised house sales were made directly as a result of a newspaper advertisement.

6) The generally high readership by women of 'Want-Ads' illustrates the strength of the market, as does the high readership and active participation by AB class readers.

7) The community purchasing the widest variety of goods (age group 35-44) is in evidence, throughout the survey, and this factor, coupled with the high AB class participation indicates an acceptance of the evening newspaper which justifies its full recognition.

8) Seventy per cent of readers have a television set in the home—yet in these homes readership of 'Want-Ads' is twenty per cent higher than in homes without television.

a) The readership of advertisements is shown to be higher on Monday than on any other evening in the week (sixty-three per cent of readers read at least one section of 'Want-Ads'). Next in order of intensity are Friday sixty-two per cent, Saturday sixty-one per cent, Tuesday fifty-nine per cent.

b) Forty-seven per cent of our readers did not go away for a holiday in 1958. (A stay-at-home market with purchasing power already higher than average, temporarily inflated by 'holidays-with-pay'.) A market that is in a mood to buy, either for the home or garden, or for leisure pursuits.'

Regionals identified the need to have a corporate body to represent their collective interests and formed the Evening Newspaper Advertising Bureau in 1962 and the Weekly Newspaper Advertising Bureau in 1966. They aimed at presenting the unique advantages of regionals to advertising agents and major clients direct as one loud central voice instead of fragmented whispers which was time-consuming to media buyers. These organisations have been exceptionally successful, and are backed by a high majority of membership. Nationals envy these corporate bodies and it would appear that they may be taking belated steps to emulate them if their own great degree of competitiveness will permit.

Advertising agents efficiently act as a supremo in buying space on behalf of their clients. Quite rightly it is the same principle as that of a manufacturer buying raw materials at the keenest price to ensure their own goods are ultimately priced competitively. Naturally, advertising agents have an unquenchable thirst for meaningful research of all the media worth considering for clients' appropriations. Statistically major regional evenings took a significant step forward in 1969 by linking with JICNARS (Joint Industry Committee for National Readership Surveys) to provide full details of readership profiles. This was guided by ENAB, and the results were whole-heartedly welcomed by advertising agents and advertisers. Exceptions prove the rule and one concedes that this research followed the lead of national newspapers. It revealed many interesting plus factors in favour of regional evenings including readership per copy averaging 2.6, a high percentage of solus daily readership up to twenty-seven per cent, that the readership profile of evenings matched very closely the adult population profile of the country itself.

It is true in the case of the regional evenings that circulation has slipped back a little in the majority of cases. This is bad and so unnecessary and is identical to the overall pattern of national newspapers. The regional evenings index has dropped from 100 to 94 in five years 1971 to 1976, as can be seen in Table 12.1.

The regional evenings index was spared a further half a per cent drop by *Express & Star/Shropshire Star* rising from 290000 to 321000 in that time, (currently up to 324000) and proving that by investing in the product with the aid of latest

Year	London Evenings		Regional Evenings		Total Evenings		London Evenings Share	
	000	Index	000	Index	000	Index	%	Index
1971	1514	100	6668	100	8182	100	18.5	100
1972	1420	94	6687	100	8107	99	17.5	94
1973	1381	91	6589	99	7970	97	17.3	94
1974	1340	89	6665	100	8005	98	16.7	90
1975	1136	75	6488	97	7624	93	14.9	81
1976	1005	66	6237	94	7242	89	13.9	75

SOURCE: ENAB   *Note* All circulation figures January-June

Table 12.1 London and regional evening circulations, 1971-7

technology, regionals could go forward and not backwards. The secret is the affinity with which regionals can get so much closer to the needs of their readers. Editionising news and advertisements is just one facet which allows flexible page sizing for each edition, and also the option of changing many other news pages throughout all editions.

Another weapon in the armoury is circulation drives backed by vigorous promotions, which bring the staff of a regional directly in contact with present and potential readers. This kind of affinity adds dimensions to the pulling power of all advertisements, because there is local involvement. All this activity is a plus factor in favour of the regionals.

Fleet Street is trying to come to terms with modern technology, but the regionals have it now.

In conclusion, Southern Publisher, do not take these 2000 words too personally because I also have 'hang-ups' regarding accountants, and believe that the ultimate mecca of some financial wizards is the achievement of asset stripping.

Here's to marketing stripping.

13   Selling circulation

JIM BROWN

Circulation Director, Manchester Evening News

Jim Brown is a former Beaverbrook journalist and Thomson Regional Newspapers manager. In 1976 his paper won the international prize of the International Circulation Managers' Association. In 1977 he collected the ICMA's award for the best sales programme at their conference in Houston, Texas.

The day of the circulation man is here. The rough and tough 'distribution fellow' who used to look after van drivers and vendors is now the sophisticated linchpin of any newspaper operation.

Successive price increases mean that newspaper sales make a massive contribution to any paper's revenue—the *Manchester Evening News* is aiming for £6.5 million this year—and unless readers can be persuaded to stay with a title then the advertising department will have a thin story to tell.

Gone is the old image of newspapers sold by vans endlessly hurtling to crumpled figures operating behind sleazy orange boxes. It was never true, but the image seemed acceptable when there were no competing television or local radio and even a Derby result ensured queues of excited buyers. Price increases, which happened every four or five years, were once feared—now they are an accepted part of any circulation man's work. The *Manchester Evening News* moved from 6p to 8p in six months and of course, the *Guardian* and *Times* both recently went straight from 12p to 15p.

Tough—yes. But regional papers are flourishing and successfully serve their dynamic markets in an age of accelerating technology and social change...only because they have introduced 'market concept'—product planning, promoting, distributing and servicing.

Circulation now use trained salesmen—the *Manchester Evening News* representatives spend many hours in the classroom every year. They are aware of the need to identify street by street, and indeed house by house, who buys the paper, then find those who do not and overcome their resistance.

The computer plays a vital role in our sales performance and forecasting. It feeds, to every branch office and representative, the sales adds or losses at every newsagent and vendor and gives individual and area comparisons against the previous week. Problem newsagents can be spotted at a glance.

We further harness technology by fitting our city vans with radios so that they can be directed to any newsagent or vendor who is in danger of selling out—average delivery time to an agent on receiving his phone call is about four minutes.

Like many other regionals, the *Manchester Evening News* has a heavy commitment in canvassing—teams of part-timers call on the door-step and telephone house-holders. In the past three years we have reached a million homes and converted over 100000 of these to having the *Evening News* delivered. The reason why home delivery is attractive—about sixty per cent of the *Manchester Evening News* goes through the letterbox every night—is that you know you have a guaranteed sale and are not subject to the vagaries of mood or weather. It also establishes habit buying—often the reader reaches out for his daily paper as much out of a need for a security blanket as for news.

The old-fashioned newsagent—particularly he who pays 'High Street' rates—is now worshipfully woo-ed by saltatory salesmen representing a myriad of products. The newspaperman has successfully to persuade the retailer to give him the key counter position, carry bills on their expensive shop frontages and even allow their paper title to be spread right across the shop fascia.

In addition, the agent, and he becomes increasingly reluctant, has to be convinced of the benefits of running a complex delivery service. Newspapers are now realising the need to help the newsagent retain his teenage deliverers and the *Manchester Evening News* has recently introduced a News Ace Club (MENACES) for news boys and girls. It offers colourful catalogue prizes for any 'Ace' signing up new readers and backs all this up with incentive trips—Aces have visited a North Sea oil rig and a group of four were taken to America for a fortnight. There are 4000 Aces and they bring in well over 100 new home delivered orders every week. The club—including negotiations for trips and prizes—is entirely controlled by the circulation function.

Much research has been undertaken to make better use of the newsagent and for an appreciation of his needs. The *Manchester Evening News* arranged twelve area seminars this year to create the scene for a frank exchange of views with retailers. Even the image of the bedraggled street vendor has been changed and we are starting to house him in a specially designed sales kiosk. The kiosks provide a striking presence in the city-centre and to get this the circulation man has had to learn to negotiate with town planners, architects, engineers ... even the Department of the Environment!

Research plays a major part in circulation work. Continuous readership research goes on all the time—readers who do not want the paper are asked *why* and those who cancel are requested to give a reason. It is carefully compiled and passed on to the editor and provides general guidelines on the kind of content that interests most readers of the paper. A newspaper is many things to many people. The specific subject matter most meaningful to the majority is continually modified by individual interests as well as by changes in the society of which the newspaper is a part.

Test marketing now goes on and Circulation run special competitions for newly signed readers and make offers of 'try it for thirty days—if you don't like it we'll refund your money.' Less than two per cent ask for their cash back.

Old-fashioned razamatazz has not been forgotten and our branch offices still punch out late news and race results on the specially constructed late press machines. Purpose-built caravans, linked to head office by radio, go out to special events and football matches to print up-to-the-minute news and results. And it is all done with great pace and excitement.

The hard-nosed part of the business is cost. Distributing papers to remote population pockets is becoming ridiculously expensive. Fresh thinking has to be applied here and a growing problem area is 'returns' (unsold copies). When newsprint was cheap there was no great risk area in pushing extra papers on to counters. But with every returned copy costing about 3p in newsprint, Circulation are having to find new systems of control—without inviting sales loss.

We are in a very competitive business and to succeed in selling, Circulation cannot allow itself to be a fragmented marketing activity. Advertising ... production ... circulation ... editorial they all have a mutual need in their approach to problems. We are well away from historic departmental isolationism in our company and weekly meetings between all management ensures a unified approach to all the varied missions of the newspaper.

Our major thinking has to be directed toward the reader. If we cannot sell to enough of them, we have no advertising!

14 Media research by the regional press: one newspaper's view of why it is necessary

BOB CARTWRIGHT

When this article was written Bob Cartwright was Marketing Services Manager of the Liverpool Daily Post and Echo Ltd. He is now Managing Director of Martak Northern Ltd., a specialist audio-visual company.

Largely because so much advertising in the regional press is local, media research and the regional press have not been the closest of bed-fellows. Arguably they have not needed to be. Despite being the largest advertising medium in the UK, because of the view that the regional press's advertisers do not need research, the regional press has approached the subject of media research with some trepidation.

However, consider the facts. The market in which all media is operating is changing rapidly. Perhaps the most important change is that Manufacturers' Consumer

Advertising, which has historically been the most important source of revenue to TV and national daily newspapers, has been declining. In contrast, the real advertisement growth sector has been retail. Traditionally retail advertising has been local and one of the main sources of advertising revenue for the local press.

Within the retail sector, there has also been a growth in nationally controlled multiple chains. These multiples, unlike some local retailers, are faced with a wide choice of media—local and national press. TV and radio. The national media are armed with at least some of the facts to demonstrate why retail advertising should be in their media. It is therefore essential that the regional press is equally armed with their own research, and soundly based arguments to prove the effectiveness of the regional medium.

However with a few honourable exceptions, the regional press has been backward in coming forward with the facts, despite the changing market situation. This is in contrast to the situation in Europe where, as David Aitchison pointed out in an article in *Marketing,* many European countries research their regional press in very considerable depth. The Norwegians, for example, are reporting on 154 titles in 104 trade districts, and even though the provision of data is expensive because the total sample needed is very large indeed, the pressure to have this information comes mainly from the newspapers themselves, and not from the advertising agencies.

So, apart from certain exceptions, why has the research effort in Britain's regional press been somewhat limited? After all, it is no more difficult for the regional press to research its markets than for the national media, some of which, such as TV and radio, are made up of regionally based companies.

The *Liverpool Echo* has in the last few years organised a number of research surveys, as have a small number of other regional papers. Liverpool's target has largely been the growing retail sector, and much of the planned research effort over the next year or so will also be pitched at this important part of the market. We feel that there is little reason why individual regional newspapers should not be pushing ahead to prove the case for the regional medium against national media, who in their turn will be trying to prove the case against the regionals now that the two are in direct competition in the retail sector, which now constitutes such a large and growing sector of the total advertising market.

Liverpool's major research effort began in 1973, following up an important 1971 study in Teesside conducted by Thomson Regional Newspapers. Both the Teesside and Liverpool studies approached the question of advertising effectiveness from the qualitative angle rather than the more heavily researched quantitative measure of cover. It is of course recognised that, in cost per thousand terms, advertising in the regional press is more expensive. The much repeated argument against this cost disadvantage was that regional evening newspapers were more effective in terms of cost per thousand buyers, and the qualitative advantages of the medium outweigh the quantitative disadvantages. It is an easy claim for the regionals to make, along with other such generalisations, albeit true ones, such as 'All sales are local'. The problem facing the regionals had been to prove that the cost disadvantages could be overcome, and that this and the combination of extra administration, production, and possibly greater creative costs can be more than counter-balanced by extra profits through the till.

The early Thomson and *Liverpool Echo* studies in 1971 and 1973 went a considerable way to supporting the qualitative strengths of the regional press. A further survey, conducted by Research Services Limited in 1975 for the *Liverpool Echo,* went into much greater detail in thirty-six product areas, and once again supported the qualitative strengths of the regional press is almost all of these product areas.

However, comparing qualitative with quantitative studies, and coverting both to a comparable cost effectiveness, is full of its own difficulties. How does an 'attitude' compare with a 'cost-per-thousand readers'? Indeed, how do both relate back to the basic objective of advertising, particularly in the retail sector, of profitably converting potential customers into actual customers?

With these problems in mind, and a continuing awareness of the ever-growing importance of retail advertising, in the autumn of last year the *Liverpool Echo* and the *Manchester Evening News* jointly commissioned Research Services Limited:

> 'To compare the effectiveness of retail store advertising for national multiples in national daily newspapers with the same advertising in regional evening newspapers.'

A number of nationally known retail companies were approached, all of whom were running National Daily schedules in the autumn of 1976. Three agreed to take equivalent space in the *Liverpool Echo* and the *Manchester Evening News,* using a sequence of three different advertisements over a period of six weeks. In principle, the survey design consisted of placing three different advertisements for a given multiple on the same day in the *Liverpool Echo,* the *Manchester Evening News* and one or more national dailies. On two subsequent days, the same three advertisements would be rotated between these publications. This would be repeated for each of the three multiple outlets involved in the exercise.

Informants were interviewed as they entered the stores in question, to assess their purchase intentions (each advertisement in the various media was promoting different merchandise); their recall and recognition of advertising for that store; their readership of regional and national dailies.

The effectiveness of the advertising in different media categories could be deduced in a number of different ways: firstly the readership patterns of shoppers in a store after the advertisements appeared, which should show a movement compared with the normal readership patterns towards those media in which the advertisements appeared; secondly, advertisement recall and recognition, which are useful indirect measures of relative advertising effectiveness, but which need to be verified against claimed readership data; and finally, the sales data provided by the retailers during the experimental period, comparing sales in those stores within the circulation area of the regional newspapers with other areas not affected by the regional newspaper advertising. In all, 3246 interviews were conducted. However, with hindsight, we recognise that the scale of the survey was so great that considerable problems were encountered in carrying out the survey to the original design. These problems mean that the results are not conclusive but, as this was one of the first surveys of its kind, they are still of considerable interest. Indeed, they are so encouraging that further research in this field is planned for 1978.

In the meantime, a number of tentative conclusions can be drawn from this complex survey.

Firstly, the response to retail advertisements amongst regional newspaper readers is equal to or greater than the response from readers of national daily newspapers and this difference widens as the content and creative element of the advertising changes. When advertisements are run stressing price reductions and special sale events, the research suggested that the response per reader was almost fifty per cent greater to advertisements in regional newspapers than to advertisements in national newspapers.

Secondly, when measured in terms of recall of advertisements, there was three times the level of recall from regional newspapers compared with national newspapers.

Thirdly, when the sales results of the stores concerned were analysed, there was a substantial increase in store traffic and turnover in those areas where regional advertisements were run as well as national advertisements, compared with other areas which were only exposed to the national advertisements.

As one can see from the activity in Liverpool, Manchester, Teesside and elsewhere, there has been some considerable effort by some regional newspapers to research their market, to establish their strengths and overcome any weaknesses. The view, most certainly in Liverpool, is that this is a worthwhile and necessary effort, because while the cash register is and will remain an important measure of advertising effectiveness for local advertisers, this has to be supplemented by well-conducted, and strongly promoted, research. After all, the cash register only works as a measure for existing customers. Surely no medium, whether national, regional or local feels every potential advertiser is an actual advertiser?

Liverpool's research effort has continued therefore, the most recent study being a survey of how people buy cars, both new and second-hand, and their use of the various media during the purchase decision. Again, the strength of the local medium, the regional evening newspaper, was confirmed.

In terms of assessing the results of such activity, it is still very early days, given that when the *Liverpool Echo* decided upon a vigorous research and promotional programme at a national level, it was accepted that the task had to be seen as long-term. But in considering whether it is a worthwhile policy, whether for Liverpool or any other regional considering existing or future research programmes, the results in commercial terms have to be continually reassessed. After all, while research can be as easy to set up for a regional newspaper as for a national medium, it is costly and therefore requires justification.

To consider the results to date, one has to remember the size of the task. That is to alter the existing custom and practice of national manufacturing and retail concerns to a conviction that it is necessary substantially to increase their expenditure to capitalise on the latent advantages of the local medium. Such conviction will only take place relatively slowly, but the signs are that the mood is changing. National advertisers are listening and taking notice of the arguments now being developed in Liverpool and elsewhere, and that has been made possible by and large because of the existence of properly conducted media research. While we would be cautious in our assessment of hard results in terms of additional business, we are encouraged by our own research findings, and by the growing interest shown by those whom we seek to convert. The interest is there, only time and continued effort will convert that interest into action.

15 New ideas on the marketing of newspapers

M. P. DOYLE

Marketing Director, South Eastern Newspapers Ltd.

J. C. THOMPSON

Managing Director, South Eastern Newspapers Ltd.

As most of us are aware the next ten years will see the evolvement of a much wider range of media, typical of which are Teletext, already available, and Viewdata, shortly to go on public trial. The breakthrough in mini-computers now means that the visual display unit, already a standard piece of equipment with many commercial enterprises, will become just as important a medium with consumers. In short, the development of the television screen, as we know it, has infinite possibilities all of which pose quite a challenge to today's conventional form of reading, whether it be books or newspapers.

We were warned 'Television? No good will come of this device. The word is half Latin and half Greek.' It would be interesting to know if C.P. Scott wrote off TV as a competitor, as all of Fleet Street did, with those words, or did he see the potential and therefore the threat to newspapers? The point is academic, as there can be no doubt that the relationship between reader and newspaper has now to be structured on a different basis to that which has held for years.

Local newspapers are in the strongest position of all press media to compete on equal terms with electronic media forms; in fact they are so uniquely placed that it is both feasible and viable for them (i.e. the newspapers) to integrate some of the development opportunities within their own product mix. The single most important asset and therefore the strength that must be developed further is the special relationship that exists between the reader and the local paper.

Dr Simon Broadbent in his foreword to the *Qualitative Role of Evening Newspapers,* a report prepared by Interscan on behalf of Thomson regionals in 1971, passed the following opinions:

> 'Our first conclusion must be that the local paper has an important and valued role within the community it serves...The second conclusion is that the local paper is read in a different way and for different reasons ... what strikes me most about the results in this report is the weakness it indicates in such *(Mirror, Sun* and *Express)* popular national newspapers. Under such headings as 'helpful', 'friendly', 'most helpful advice' and 'enjoyable' the evening newspaper is head and shoulders above the popular national newspapers.'

These latter comments, fully quantified in the survey, were in a sense, expanded upon by the *Liverpool Daily Post and Echo* who, together with Research Services Ltd, in their surveys *The Role of the Media in Consumer Buying Decision* and *Attitudes to Media in the New Merseyside,* see the results shown in Table 15.1. The juxtapositioning of these extracts is

	TV %	National Daily %	Local Evening Newspaper %
Media whose advertising is most useful	16	10	32
Media giving most helpful information in ordinary everyday life	21	26	20
Which of the two (press) media is most useful		28	63
Media whose advertising is trusted most	19	7	28

Ref:
Attitudes to Media in the New Merseyside (Liverpool Daily Post & Echo—1970) The Role of Media in Consumer Buying Decisions (Liverpool Daily Post & Echo—1976).

Table 15.1 Attitudes to local media

deliberate in that the final conclusion, albeit inferential, is that the special relationship we claim to enjoy, is one which can be borne out by evidence.

Thus new ideas on the marketing of (local) newspapers stem from this unique association with our public and in the long term obviously must be geared toward consolidating the relationship.

For reasons which become apparent, the distributive aspect of newspaper marketing must be freed from the existing outlet monopoly of newsagents. Already a number of 'modern' evening newspapers operate a direct delivery system of their own, whereby the canvassing of customers, delivery and charging is entirely the publisher's responsibility. At the moment approximately sixty-five per cent of all local evening sales are delivered copies, managed either by the newsagents or the paper direct. The new evening newspapers have a higher proportion of delivered copies under their own control.

It follows therefore that an essential prerequisite in the re-positioning of newspapers is the consolidation of this direct contact by the publishing representative (the delivery boy/girl) with the customer. It is from here that a new rapport can be developed.

A classic example of how, for whom, and specific only to local papers, is the Ladies Readership Clubs. At the moment sixteen local evening newspapers have such a club. In our own area, Medway, we have 12000-plus members affiliated to the *Kent Evening Post* through Oasis (the ladies club) who in the course of the year are propositioned with up to 150 activities ranging from cookery demonstrations to holidays in Japan. In order to underpin this key feature we are widening the appeal, backed by four editorial pages per week, to the family as a whole, supported by an Oasis road show which will be taken around the area during the year.

Furthermore we will be producing a quarterly magazine containing photographs, news and views of members, supported by comment on local trade including details of the latest Oasis special offer. The publication will come in their quarterly sample parcel which will contain just that—samples of products. Setting aside the product testing advantages offered, the concept is designed to 'lock-in' readers, i.e. members of the circle, to our publication. In that respect we are currently working on an introduction of 'contracted readers' to the *Kent Evening Post,* identified by their willingness to pre-pay or authorise a bankers order.

The extension of this very close relationship with readers could be further facilitated by opening up schemes, such as group insurance, bulk buying, car buying and other activities. The opportunities are many and varied. Obviously all of our 'recognised' buyers will be held on computer so that access can be gained speedily and in line with specific market requirements.

In the context of data banks, we also envisage being in a position to aid advertisers by utilising further the computer hardware which, with large numbers of local newspapers, is

currently used for setting purposes. Within the next year or so
it should be possible for an advertiser, when contracting to
buy space, to be offered a proportionate amount of time on a
computer. Branch offices would hold a VDU from which the
customer could call up whatever information he or she
requires, at a nominal price. All part of the new wider local
newspaper service—competing with the Viewdata and
Teletext type of system, employing their skills but trading on
the already established customer belief, confidence and trust
in their local medium.

As to the cosmetics and packaging as a whole, then it
becomes a matter of personal choice. We, for our part,
operate a continual evaluation of our products, out of which
has come the decision to go tabloid with two of our weeklies
and the raising of cover prices by over fifty per cent in the
past two years. The fact that our circulation for 1976 was the
highest in the company's history and that financially we have
guaranteed sufficient funds for capital replacement with
tomorrow's needs in mind, suggests that our judgment is
reasonable. Our view is that newspapers in the future have to
be constructed far more logically than at present. In that
regard cognisance of the multiplicity of interests shared
amongst the average household, together with different uses
required of the paper, suggest to us that the newspaper of
tomorrow must be packaged to meet those specific target
needs.

We intend to introduce a further element which will be
based on commercially-oriented information but made up in
easily identifiable segments. Why advertising-oriented
information? We know that classified is the second most, if
not *the* most read part of the paper (ref *Qualitative Role of
Newspapers*—1971) and therefore advertising of that genre
will be adding to the volume of information carried. The
nature of this matter is not original, it is similâr to the Allison
Grey by-line type of format, but in the context of local
newspapers it is something of an innovation. Particularly, it
will be contained in a supplement of its own, with each page
geared to each member of the family. Thus the structure of

	1972	1973	1974	1975	1976
National Newspapers	18.4	18.3	17.8	16.8	16.6
Television	24.9	24.0	22.6	24.4	25.8
Regional Newspapers	26.5	29.3	30.4	29.2	27.6

Source: *Advertising Association*

Table 15.2 Percentage of total advertising expenditure by media

the total newspaper package is one designed to meet, instantly, the average household needs and the infrastructure of at least one part of the package is designed also with that in mind.

Brand navigation, in terms of local newspapers, will be successful, provided publishers fully understand the nature of the unique bond which exists between them and their readers. Also, they, the publishers, must work *with* the electronic forms of communication and not against them. As regards the advertiser, nationally local press is ignored for reasons almost wholly connected with London advertising agencies and their myopic approach to campaign planning, perhaps summed up by the inane comment of one media director: 'The Press? That's something I threaten the other media with'.

It is a tragedy, at least for the advertiser, because the local press medium is one which can produce results. The evidence is there. In the years 1972-6, regional newspapers had the highest share of advertising expenditure (see Table 15.2), the cornerstone of which was classified ('the bedrock of the press'—McLuhan) a category of business that expands only if successful. In short we get results because our readers are that interested.

Cost per mille comparisons should start there: the reason they cannot is because information on effect is lacking in other media, not ours.

We know our markets and they know us. The bond between readers and their local newspapers stems from immovable characteristics of trust, loyalty, confidence and credibility.

Regional newspapers are part of an 'evolving communication process. Having already demonstrated our willingness and ability to work with computer technology in the production field, it is now a matter of harnessing that which is relevant form the new technologies to re-enforcing the unique association we enjoy with our customers. At the same time never lose sight of the fact that the real magic of the regional press, consistent with all press, is the fact that it is print ...

16 Co-partnership — a regional press innovation

DOUGLAS L. BIRD

Group Sales Manager, Eastern Counties Newspapers

When this article was written Douglas Bird was on secondment to the Evening Newspaper Advertising Bureau, his brief being to test the viability of the concept of Co-partnership in this country and, should it prove successful, to set up a department to run it. This has now been achieved.

Advertising itself is not important, but moving the product is. Co-partnership—a new service provided by ENAB (Evening Newspaper Advertising Bureau) is a marketing concept designed to offer sales benefits as well as advertising advantages. It is designed to provide manufacturers with a tool to encourage product movement through increased merchandising and promotional activity on the part of the retailer. Co-partnership also makes it possible for national advertisers to harness the effectiveness of regional and local advertising without the problems traditionally associated with this fragmented medium.

Successful local retailers know that advertising works. If it were not so they would not use it so frequently. They know that good local advertising will bring customers into their store and increase their stock-turn. Consequently, it is possible for a manufacturer to influence retail buying decisions by offering attractive advertising opportunities, enabling retailers to increase their own promotional efforts.

If the retailer is to be influenced by a promotion, it must be in a form attractive to him. The traditional fifty/fifty dealer block approach to co-operative advertising does not often excite the retailer sufficiently to persuade him to change his buying policy. He is not sufficiently impressed with the opportunity to put his name and address under an ad which is at least eighty per cent manufacturer dominated, for which he has to pay fifty per cent of the cost, only to find competing stores using the same ad.

Co-partnership is attractive to the retailer because it presents him with a flexible advertising allowance which he can build into his own campaigns and use to mount his own promotions. This principle has in recent years become widely adopted in America. Normal procedure is for the retailer to be offered copy elements or components, which might consist of the manufacturer's logo, product illustration and perhaps a headline or suggested copy, so that the retailer's ad ties in which the manufacturer's national campaign.

One reason why this practice has developed in the States has been the involvement of the newspaper, and this is the facility that ENAB now offers in Great Britain. Each member newspaper has appointed a co-ordinator who, briefed by ENAB with details of the manufacturer's offer, has representatives to contact the retailers and a studio to prepare the ads.

Giving this flexibility to the retailer may mean some loss of advertising control, but co-partnership should not be viewed simply as a method of advertising, but rather as a selling or marketing tool: a means of moving the product. The benefits that lie in these areas more than outweigh and loss of advertising control.

With these objectives in mind, most American dealer programmes are based on accrual systems whereby the retailer is given the advertising allowance in direct relation to the value of goods purchased. Accruals may range from an allowance of one per cent of purchases, to anything up to fifteen per cent, but, of course, the retailer only gets the money after he can prove that he has spent it. This ensures that the allowance is spent actually promoting the goods and not on price-cutting or on the retailer's Spanish holiday or any other area which is non-productive for the manufacturer.

Whilst most programmes are pitched around the two per cent to five per cent mark, one of the most successful has been the Parke Davis Pharmaceutical offer to pay the full cost of retailer advertising for their product up to the value of fifteen per cent of purchases. Naturally, newspaper salesmen throughout America have been calling on drug stores, supermarkets and all Parke Davis outlets pointing out to them that by buying Parke Davis rather than competing brands, they can place an individually prepared advertising campaign in their local paper free of charge. In each of the last three years Parke Davis have increased their level of accruals as they have found how successful this kind of promotion can be.

Another American company, Simmons Bedding, have used an accrual-based co-op programme to achieve better in-store display. They have offered stockists two per cent accruals providing they display at least six of various beds in their range. Then they offer a bonus plan whereby the dealer gets three per cent accruals if he displays ten beds and finally, a premium plan where they offer four per cent in return for fourteen beds. That is simply a means of buying floor space.

The major potential benefits of co-partnership for the manufacturer can be summarised under four headings:

(1) The retailer has an incentive to buy-in more of the product at the expense of competing brands, in order to gain higher advertising contributions.

(2) The newspaper sales forces, by pointing out to the retailer the advantages of buying that particular product in order to gain the advertising allowance, indirectly help the manufacturer to sell-in.

(3) The retailer, having bought-in more of the product and agreed to advertise it, will give the product good in-store display.

(4) Local advertising placed by the retailer then appears to move the goods out to the consumer.

In this country most manufacturers spend their money in two ways. Firstly, below-the-line incentives or discounts in order to get the goods stocked and, secondly, national advertising, to create brand image and product awareness. The hole in this mix is local promotion at the point of sale, and co-partnership presents a means of filling this gap.

Viewed as a sales and marketing tool, cost per thousand considerations are largely irrelevant and co-partnership should be compared not with national advertising media, but with alternative means of achieving retailer involvement and point of sale promotion. Equally, with the retailer responsible for placing the campaign, and with the assistance of the newspaper for preparing the advertising, the administrative and production problems of the regional press are also overcome.

Recent qualitative research has supported the belief that advertising in regional evenings is more sales effective than indicated by straight quantitative research. Co-partnership now presents a method of making the most of this effectiveness whilst at the same time offering considerable selling benefits. Already a number of manufacturers have conducted successful tests using Co-partnership and a department is now being established at ENAB to provide the complete service necessary for its undoubted potential to be fulfilled.

PART V

Consumer magazines

17 Magazines, markets and money

MICHAEL BIRD

Marketing Director, National Magazine Company Ltd.

In one or two important ways newspapers and magazines are different.

The dramatic confrontations that Jocelyn Stevens has been having with *Daily Express* printing workers in recent years are quite unlike anything that he faced when he was the publisher/proprietor of the *Queen*. For one thing, the *Queen* did not have its printing-press downstairs, and even if it had, the prospect of its stopping for a few days would not have threatened its survival; if its survival was ever threatened by anything, politicians and commentators on matters of national interest certainly did not talk earnestly about the problems of the magazine industry as an indispensable part of our priceless heritage of a free press, in need of subsidy or other intervention. For which differences magazine publishers are no doubt heartily grateful. Magazines stay in being because their customers want them; it they do not want a magazine sufficiently strongly, it goes and its place is taken by others. British magazines are free of the burdens and the privileges of being national institutions in the eyes of leader-writers or politicians. However personally idealistic magazine journalists may be, magazines live and die in a wholly commercial environment.

Newspaper offices are like factories; magazine offices are like advertising agencies. Newspapers have immense investments in plant—and all the accompanying problems; the assets of a magazine company catch the six o'clock train home every night. National newspapers print in London; magazines print anywhere but in London.

In short, magazine publishers are freer to start, stop or change direction. Any entrepreneur[1] can set up in business as a magazine publisher (which keeps the existing publishers on their toes) though whether they can continue in business and make a living is another question. How magazines make a living is what this paper is about.

The role of magazines

It is easy to say what magazines do for their readers, until one is asked, 'Yes, but what do they do that other media *don't* do? What do they do much *better* than other media?' Since the list of claimed areas of superiority might run into hundreds of specific items, let us attempt a general, almost philosophical view.

The more frequently a print medium is published, the greater its immediacy, but the lower its reference-value:

High immediacy —————————————— *High reference value*

Daily newspapers	Weekly newspapers	Weekly magazines	Monthly magazines	Part-works	Paper-back books	Hard-back books

Short physical life —————————————— *Long physical life*

---

[1] The classic definition of an entrepreneur being someone who takes risks with other people's money.

Obviously, the extent of immediacy/reference value also determines the length of time a publication is retained, which in turn is related to the extent of repeat-readership and of multiple readers-per-copy. The strength of magazines is that they combine authority with topicality at a low price. A problem which magazines face however is that on the one side they cannot directly compete with newspapers in immediacy, nor on the other side can they compete with books in reference-value. The problem is heightened by the fact that newspapers are acquiring improved capacity for colour reproduction, and are carrying increasing amounts of 'magazine' content, ie. feature material in which the date is almost irrelevant. On the other side magazines have to compete not only with hardback books but with paperbacks and partworks, which lay claim to the authority and reference-value of books, while being marketed as aggressively, if not more aggressively, than magazines, through mass outlets with the aid of mass promotion.

Of course the spectrum can be extended further towards the left: the medium that has greatest immediacy and the shortest life[2] is—of course—television. Television pre-empts so much of the traditional editorial role of newspapers that the latter have occupied much of the traditional editorial preserve of magazines—analysis, entertainment, instruction, light relaxation, stimulation of fashion and life-styles etc., etc.

What prevents magazines from being dangerously squeezed on both sides? The most important measurable factor is advertising, which in effect subsidises the editorial content of magazines and helps them to offer value for money to the reader. Thus compare a part-work, carrying no advertising, with a magazine; in physical content terms the magazine can afford to offer twice or three times the editorial pages per penny. Nevertheless the fact that partworks are successful in spite of this indicates the competitive pressure that quality reference-media, properly promoted and

---

[2] Until widespread home-videotaping makes voluntary repeat viewership practical.

distributed, can exercise on magazines. The two linked economic problems of magazines are therefore:

1. How do magazines generate advertisement revenue?
2. How can acceptable value-for-money continue to be offered to readers?

The importance of other things not being equal

The above discussion began by describing the *editorial* competition of other media. It is clear however that magazines are threatened by more rapid media on the advertising side as well. Other things being equal, advertisers prefer to get an audience all in one day and the majority prefer audio-visual media to print. They like short copy dates and regional flexibility.

The survival and prosperity of the various categories of magazines therefore largely depend on the extent to which other things are *not* equal—and on their ability to make it manifestly clear to advertisers that they are not equal.

How well in practice are magazines as a whole competing for advertisements? There is no escaping the fact that magazines' share of total advertising expenditure has declined since the 1960s (though it appears to have stabilised in the past three years). (See Table 17.1.)

Moreover, since 1970 magazines have shown the lowest increase of media rates (i.e. cost/000 circulation) of all media categories (see Table 17.2).

A number of reasons can be adduced for this (in addition to the obvious one, that magazine publishers are wholly lacking in rapacity or avarice):

(1) Government pressure has made successful magazines unable to increase rates in line with circulations and costs, while less successful ones have been forced down by

% Share of total advertising expenditure	
1960	12
1964	11
1968	10
1972	9
1976	8

Source: *Advertising Quarterly Summer 1977*

Table 17.1 Advertising in magazines and periodicals

	Indices of media rates 1970 = 100
Regional dailies	230
Weekly papers	214
Trade & technical	211
Television	*206*
National dailies	203
National Sundays	196
Magazines and periodicals	191
Retail price index	**215**

Source: *Advertising Quarterly Summer 1977*

Table 17.2 Indices of Media Rates, 1976

ordinary commercial competitive pressures. In other words free market forces have been allowed to work mainly in one way—downwards. However, this may be true to varying extents of other media categories too.

(2) Readership, rather than circulation, has been a criterion of suitability for campaigns, and in recent years till December 1976, reader-per-copy ratios had tended to slide.

(3) Demand affects price (even when governments attempt to control it). The demand for regional press advertising

space, for instance, has been greater than for magazines; and that in turn is due to some important structural changes in the pattern of advertising expenditure, in particular the trend towards retailer advertising and the growth of classified, both of which benefit newspapers, in particular regional papers.

The two main media sectors to make progress have been TV and regional newspapers, both what you might call 'regional-rapid-media'. Among magazines, in real revenue terms the mass women's weeklies have been severely affected, partly as result of the long-term decline in mass weeklies' circulations and partly because of the similarity of their readerships to the mainstream of the commercial TV audience. The advertisement-revenue earning-power of different magazines is closely related to the class/educational level of their readership and inversely related to their readers' exposure to commercial television.[3]

To talk about magazines globally, therefore, is like bracketing the *Sun, Daily Express* and *Financial Times* when discussing newspapers. Let us take a closer look at the revenues that different magazines make and at the reasons for the wide variations between them.

Where the money goes—and why

Direct comparisons of weeklies and monthlies in advertisement revenue terms are clearly invalid, because of the difference in frequency of publication. The first analysis is therefore confined to monthlies: however it throws an

---

[3] As with all sweeping statements there are exceptions: on this basis *Radio Times* ought in theory to generate more revenue per reader than *TV Times* but does not do so in practice. However such discrepancies from the general rule are usually the result of deliberate commercial policy by the publisher, relating to production, costs etc., rather than being the result of agency attitudes to the respective value of media audiences. D.C. Thomson are another case in point.

interesting light on the way media revenues are allocated.

Figure 17.1 shows how closely the revenues earned by women's monthlies are related to their number of ABC1 women readers. No other single demographic (age/class) breakdown produces such as close fit as ABC1s.[4] The correlation is in excess of 0.99. Every ABC1 woman reader is worth about £2 to the publisher per year.

The variation around the line, while small, is interesting: all but one of the magazines above the line are square-backed; all but one of the magazines *below* the line i.e. generating less than £2 per ABC1 reader per year, are saddle-stitched. Square-backed magazines look more luxurious but, more importantly, have a more flexible make-up of pages and can accommodate larger quantities of advertising in boom months, while a saddle-stitched magazine may have to turn clients away. On the other hand, the square-backed magazine is more expensive to produce. The chart is therefore not necessarily an indicator of relative profitability, but only of revenue-earning power.

For the five big women's weeklies the relationship is similar, the correlation between ABC1 class readerships and MEAL (Media Expenditure Analysis Ltd) advertisement revenue in 1976 being 0.997, while between *circulation* and revenue the correlation is only 0.782. Correlation is not causality, as we all know. The most useful function of a high correlation is to provoke us into asking 'why?'. For instance, not all magazines strive equally urgently to sell advertisement space; D.C. Thomson's[5] *My Weekly,* well down market, is presumably costed to make money on the cover price and is certainly not selling as much advertisement space as its potential; even on the basis of its relatively small profile of ABC readers *My Weekly* could in theory earn twice its

---

[4] *Educational* breaks, however, are very closely related to advertisement revenues in continental countries and the same is, on first examination, likely to be true in Britain.

[5] It is no slight on a much admired—but impossible to emulate—company that we did not telephone Dundee to ask for the secrets of D.C. Thomson. I can only quote the member of the Royal Commission who returned from Scotland exclaiming, 'I have seen the past—and it works!'.

present advertisement income.

Money therefore appears to flow into magazines very much according to the numbers of middle-class readers they deliver. This may come as a surprise to those who believe that advertising money today primarily flows towards Youth, not Class. Why the prevalence of that belief? Firstly a great deal of new product activity both by manufacturers and by publishers has attracted attention to the young sector. It is the liveliest and most responsive field for innovation. It is a less tradition-bound market that is easier for the publisher to enter (witness the fate of *Inhabit*—an attractive magazine that tackled *Ideal Home* and *Homes & Gardens* on their own territory in 1973 and expired very shortly afterwards). The successful young magazines are very upmarket anyway; little money goes into downmarket young magazines like *Loving* or *True*. It may be that we see numerous schedule analyses commissioned by agencies specifying 15-34s, but the downmarket romantic magazines are frequently not candidates. Class will out.

Class is not a wholly causal factor, but is rather a factor linked with other desirable elements from many advertisers' point of view, such as paper and print quality, specialised and authoritative editorial, large readership-per-copy, high cover price, etc. It is unlikely that the majority of magazine schedules are actually prepared with the prime object of reaching ABC1s. However, if the publisher takes actions, whether editorially or in production or pricing, which result in a more competitive cost-efficiency in reaching ABC1s, his finances are likely to be better off *pro rata*.

Revenue per copy comparisons

The advertisement revenue a magazine is capable of earning from a single copy varies from a penny to a pound. Table 17.3 shows two ranked (not exhaustive) lists of magazines. The monthlies fall into fairly neat categories, which have

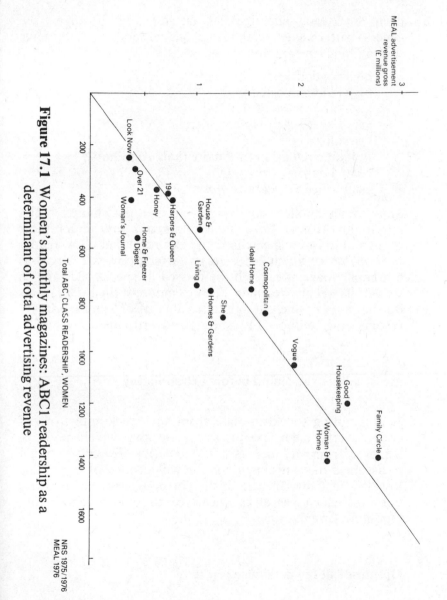

Figure 17.1 Women's monthly magazines: ABC1 readership as a determinant of total advertising revenue

been bracketed. The weeklies are less tidy: however, the general pattern emerges that the high earners (over 50p) have several things in common:

high cover price;
high readers-per-copy;
high proportion of ABC1s;
very low exposure to commercial TV;
specialised editorial;
modest circulation (not more than ⅓ million);
coated paper;
established *50 years or more.*

Many other publications have some of these characteristics but not all of them. For instance *Woman's Journal* has most of them, but is not specialised and as a result has a low reader per copy ratio, which depresses its earning-power. (*Punch,* as a humour magazine, might be classed as specialised, and in view of its weekly frequency, counts amongst the high earners on the basis of the annual cash value of a regular primary reader, which is about £12 a head in advertisement revenue.)

Please adjust your mind before extrapolating

It is tempting to extrapolate from such reckonings of per copy advertisement revenue to the earnings which might be achieved from any increases in circulation. Equally it might be assumed that falls in circulation will lead to corresponding losses in revenue. In fact this is not necessarily so; it is this question which lies at the heart of the controversy about Optimum Circulations.

Optimise sales to maximise profit

The optimum sales level of any product is the point at which

Weeklies		Monthlies		
*Country Life	84	*Vogue	101	} Fashion
*Investors Chronicle	57	*Harpers & Queen	92	
Punch	23			
Sunday Times Magazine	13	*House & Garden	75	
Observer Magazine	13	*Ideal Home	70	Home
Motor	13	*Good Housekeeping	68	interest
Autocar	12	*Homes & Gardens	53	
Woman's Own	9			
Woman	8	19	36	
Woman's Realm	8	Cosmopolitan	35	Young
TVTimes	7	She	35	magazines
Woman's Weekly	5	Over 21	30	
Radio Times	4	Honey	29	
My Weekly	3			
		Woman & Home	29	
		Family Circle	27	
		Mother	26	Other
		Homemaker	25	home
		Woman's Journal	22	and
		Living	14	general
		Home & Freezer		interest
		Digest	10	
		Sewing & Knitting	9	

* Revenue per copy of over 50p

Table 17.3 Magazines ranked in order of advertisement revenue (pence) per copy sold

the extra revenue from each additional item sold is outweighed by the extra cost. There is always some point at which either the marginal *revenue* gets smaller (e.g. prices have to be reduced in order to increase sales) or the *cost* becomes too great (you have to hire extra plant, pay overtime, waste too many unsold copies, spend more on promotion, etc.). Some of the limits, however, are purely physical: thus the 'optimum' circulation of *Woman* in 1957 was determined by the capacity of the printing presses (at a figure approaching four million) and so *Woman's Realm* was launched to meet the extra consumer and advertiser demand. Such mechanical limits are not too difficult to identify. It is more difficult to measure the *marketing* factors that place practical limits on circulation, and it is with these factors that this paper is mainly concerned. Put at its simplest the marketing factors are:

(1) The public's demand for the publication at varying prices.

(2) The amount that advertisers are prepared to pay for a space in the publication at varying circulation levels.

These factors clearly (or obscurely, in some cases) interact, and it is perhaps not surprising that the goal of making more money than one spends, over the middle and long term, has been lost to view from time to time, either by pushing circulations to ruinous heights or by rationing the printing of copies in spite of consumer demand.

This is a massive subject which needs a separate, complete article to itself, but a few brief points are worth making.

It is *not* true to say that a magazine is in trouble if the cover-price revenue (after allowing for the wholesaler's and retailer's cut of about forty-five per cent) does not exceed the marginal run-on cost per copy. However it is very true that:

1. A magazine is at risk, from competition or from a downturn on advertising, when the cover revenue fails even to pay for the marginal cost of that part of the publication which consists of editorial reading-matter. This certainly happened with *Saturday Evening Post* in the USA.

2. Selling additional copies at a run-on loss only makes sense when that 'loss' is covered by the rationally-anticipated increase in next year's advertisement revenue resulting from this year's extra circulation sales.

The convertibility of circulation increases into increases in advertisement rates (rather than into increase in *paging,* which chiefly tend to increase costs) is the central economic problem of all consumer magazines where advertisement revenue is a larger proportion of income than circulation sales.

To the extent that the convertibility of copy sales into advertisement sales of a given magazine is found to be higher or lower than the publisher thought, the optimum circulation is itself likely to be a higher or lower figure than the current level; the cover price is affected in the opposite direction. A high convertibility (or high 'elasticity'[6]) of advertisement revenue relative to circulation will therefore encourage low cover price (and conversely).

Thus, for *The Times,* the increases in circulation some years ago were not convertible *pro rata* into real increases in advertising rates: the appropriate commercial policy in response to this in elasticity was therefore one of steep increases in cover price. (See Michael Mander in Chapter 7.)

Exactly the same considerations apply with magazines. At the strictly commercial level, magazines and newspapers are not different.

High advertisement revenue/circulation elasticity: factors encouraging circulation growth and low cover price

A high elasticity (1.0 or more) for advertising revenue against circulation is not at all improbable: examples of situations in which a ten per cent increase in circulation could generate an increase in revenue of say fifteen per cent or twenty per cent would be:

---

[6] 'Elasticity' is the conventional jargon term for the response of sales to price changes. When a price increase is cancelled-out exactly by a fall in sales, so that total revenue remains unchanged, elasticity is 1.0 (strictly speaking —1.0, since sales move the opposite way to price). 'High elasticity' is normally used to refer to more than proportionate changes of sales in response to price changes. 'Advertising-circulation elasticity' is a term invented by the writer to refer to the response of advertisement demand to changes in circulation.

1. Where the advertiser's need for *coverage* is paramount
   and where cheap repetition is of low importance. It is
   known that, other things being equal, by comparison with
   smaller media, a publication with a large readership will
   make a contribution to the net coverage of a schedule that
   is *greater* than the difference in audience size: if publication *A* has a ten per cent larger audience than publication
   B it usually contributes twelve to fifteen per cent more to
   the total net audience than does publication *B*. To the
   extent that the advertiser is willing to pay a premium for
   coverage (which is generally the case) the high coverage
   medium can charge a high cost/000 and still sell the same
   number of pages.

2. Where the pressure is for 'short' schedules, i.e. small
   numbers of publications on the media list, for reasons of
   administrative convenience etc. Such pressures will
   necessarily work against the smaller publication.

(One might include in this list the potential benefit that might
accrue to the advertisement departments of some magazines
if their circulation could be boosted to the point when the
publishers could be honest and issue audited circulation,
preferably ABC, figures. Whether such publications could
afford such a policy, on the other hand, is an interesting
question; it could play havoc with the costs side of the
operation, since the publisher could then be obliged to print
at least as many copies as he is claiming to sell. A specially
fascinating field of optimisation for the technician, this one,
requiring him to calculate and correlate the nerve of the
publisher, the discretion of the printing firm and the
continuing credulity of some advertisers.)

Low advertisement revenue/circulation elasticity:
factors tending to discourage circulation growth
and encouraging high cover price

Low levels of elasticity of advertisement rate to circulation occur in the following situations:

1. When the advertisers are small, not technically sophisticated in audience research, and have limited budgets. An increase in rate may simply reduce the frequency with which they advertise, or drive them away altogether. The absolute rate is the figure they watch, not rate/000.

2. When the highly specialised advertiser knows that the audience he is trying to reach is strictly limited in number and that it represents the hard-core of the readership of the publication. He assumes that an increase of ten per cent in sale will not increase significantly the coverage of these people and that even a decrease of ten per cent would not affect it greatly, particularly if the fall in sale was brought about by a price increase which drives away only casual buyers of lower value to the advertiser.

3. When the advertiser is not necessarily highly specialised but is aiming at an audience with well-defined class/ income/age/ownership/product-usership characteristics. If this is coupled with a situation in which as circulation increase the audience profile is diluted, becoming steadily less differentiated from the population average, the advertiser will not be prepared to pay the same rate per thousand for the extra readers.

4. When the readership-per-copy tends to fall as circulation increases. In other words, when readership is itself inelastic relative to circulation. The advertisers who are interested in a competitive cost/000, whether in a specialised or a mass market, will expect rates to reflect readership changes, not circulation. Again, the rate cannot increase *pro rata* to circulation. This tendency of readership per copy to decline with increasing sale, coupled with dilution of the audience profile, is the main cause of low advertisement rate/circulation elasticity.

All these factors tend to combine, particularly with magazines that have a large audience but a specialised character such as *Vogue, Ideal Home* and *Good Housekeeping,* where the range of advertisers is vast and their motives for using the medium diverse. However it is in principle feasible to break down the client list and categorise them broadly in different groups, ranking them by their likely sensitivity to changes in, respectively, the circulation figure, the readership profile, the total audience, etc., and to weight the groups by their respective contribution to the magazine's revenue. From such a study a more precise estimate of advertisement rate/circulation elasticity can be derived.

There is an irony here: careful study of these propositions concerning advertisement-circulation elasticity indicates that the women's weeklies could profitably use the extra circulation but have not been getting it: monthlies need circulation growth much less urgently, but have been getting it anyway. Dr Malthus, thou shouldst be living at this hour.

18 The economics of the TV Times

JEREMY POTTER

Managing Director, Independent Television Publications Limited

Jeremy Potter has been Managing Director of Independent Television Publications Limited since the beginning of 1970. Before that he was Managing Director and Deputy Chairman of the New Statesman. He is a Vice-President of the Periodical Publishers Association and Chairman of its Management Committee.

A salient feature of *TVTimes* is its uncategorisability. It is a programme journal. It is a family magazine. It is a mass-market gravure publication which is topical and neither up-market nor down-market. It is among the largest of press media, but wholly owned by television interests. It is the only word in the English language which begins with three capital letters. As for its economics, they too are improbable. I have been grappling with them for three-quarters of a decade with undiminishing astonishment—sometimes grasping them firmly, like nettles, but still getting stung; sometimes fingering a loose connection gingerly and retiring in a state of shock.

Every week we have to concoct, print, distribute and sell 3.6 million copies in thirteen separate editions. The production schedule for each issue covers a period of six weeks and, owing to the number of pages changed between editions, a ninety-six-page issue can involve more than 300 pages. In the course of a year we use more than 40000 tonnes of paper. The need for topicality in programme information necessitates a tight schedule, but accuracy and a high standard of printing are essential too. Printing is in two sections to allow the maximum time for late copy changes. Distribution is made to some 30000 newsagents via 400 wholesalers and, as *TVTimes* has a normal shop life of only three or four days, there can be no delay without loss of sales.

Unlike Gaul, publishers fall into only two parts: publishers pure and simple and publishers who are printers as well. Unusually for such a large-scale operation, we are pure and simple, and our economics are therefore unaffected when there is spare capacity and the hungry machines look up and are not fed. Our own staff is remarkably small; 218 people look after *TVTimes, Look-in* and all our extras, books and subsidiary frolics. Between us last year we generated a total turnover of £24 million. Thus, at more than £100000 per person, we must be doing almost as well as an advertising agency.

Revenue

Like the rest of the press but unlike most mass-market products, *TVTimes* has two sources of revenue: from copy sales and from advertisements. The breakdown over the past eight years is shown in Table 18.1.

The sales figures represent only part of what the readers pay for *TVTimes*. In the year which ended in July 1977, for instance, the amount retained by the wholesale and retail

Year Ending July	Net Sales Revenue £'000	Index	Net Advertisement Revenue £'000	Index
1970	3,721	100	3,108	100
1971	4,692	126	3,356	108
1972	5,145	138	3,634	117
1973	5,876	158	4,690	151
1974	6,957	187	5,999	193
1975*	8,218	221	5,161	166
1976	10,611	285	7,720	248
1977	12,607	339	9,751	314

* revenues affected by a printer's strike

Table 18.1 TVTimes' revenue, 1970-77

trade totalled almost £9 million. Similarly, the figure of £9 751 000 advertisement revenue does not represent the full amount paid by advertisers, agencies retaining some £1.75 million.

Sales

According to the latest JICNARS (Joint Industry Committee for National Readership Survey) figures, *TVTimes* had nearly 1.6 million more readers in the first six months of 1977 compared to the first six months of 1976. Adult readers now total 11 203 000. This is the largest magazine readership in Britain, and to it should be added some two million children.

Sales of the various editions differ widely. First comes the London edition, not far behind the two London evening newspapers put together. Last come the Grampian and Border editions whose quantities on their own would never justify gravure printing. Indeed each edition is a story in itself. For example, with its weekly page in Welsh, the HTV edition has disseminated the Welsh language more widely than any other medium since the first Celt picked up his first

London	816,011	Tyne Tees	155,931
ATV	492,801	Scottish TV	146,593
Granada	430,084	Westward	128,192
Yorkshire	370,335	Ulster	102,603
Southern	307,168	Grampian	46,482
HTV	269,444	Border	38,073
Anglia	185,854	**Total**	**3,489,571**

Table 18.2 Breakdown of TVTimes' sales, by editions

harp. The breakdown of sales by editions (January-June 1977) is shown in Table 18.2.

Advertisements

Growth in advertisement revenue has reached the point at which eleven consecutive issues this autumn were fully booked to the present maximum size of ninety-six pages. This steady increase in the volume of advertising and hence in the size of issues has been a critical factor in the economics of *TVTimes*. In 1970 the average size of issue was fifty-six pages; in 1976 it was seventy-six pages. Over this period the average number of national advertisement pages per issue rose form 18.5 to 34.8, while the average number of colour pages has almost trebled. Indeed only concentration on selling colour has kept revenue ahead of costs, and colour now accounts for two-thirds of advertisement revenue. In contrast, regional advertising is financially less attractive to us than national and has not kept pace. In 1970 it accounted for twenty-five per cent of the whole; by 1976 this had dropped to eight per cent. The breakdown of gross advertisement revenue for 1976 is shown in Table 18.3.

All product categories are represented among *TVTimes* advertisements, and it may be of interest to compare the relative distribution of categories between *TVTimes* and

	(£'s)	%
National colour	6,537,223	64.2
National mono	2,832,746	27.8
Regional colour	240,931	2.4
Regional mono	565,243	5.6
	10,176,143	100.0

Table 18.3 TVTimes' gross advertisement revenue, 1976

	TVTimes %	Television %
Retail & mail order	20.5	7.5
Tobacco	18.2	1.5
Household goods	13.2	14.7
Drink	10.8	9.1
Leisure & entertainment	6.2	5.6
Wearing apparel	5.7	2.1
Food	5.2	29.0
Holidays travel & transport	3.5	2.2
Motors	3.5	3.9
Government & service	3.2	2.0
Financial	2.5	1.8
Pharmaceutical	2.4	3.5
Publishing	1.6	3.0
Toiletries & cosmetics	1.2	9.7
Institutional & industrial	1.1	1.4
Agriculture & horticulture	0.7	0.3
Charity, educational societies	0.5	-
Office equipment	0.2	0.2
Local advertisers	*	2.6
	100	100

*not separately recorded

Table 18.4 Distribution of advertisement revenue, TVTimes and television

television for 1976 (see Table 18.4). This serves to underline the fact that *TVTimes* has developed into a prime advertisement medium in its own right independent of its television connection and not closely related to other colour press media (newspaper supplements, women's magazines), nor to those few newspapers whose readership is similar in size (but different in kind, and for the most part not able to offer colour).

Costs

Growth in revenue must be seen in the context of inflation, for growth in costs has been sensational too. Most notably, there has been a sky-high rise in the cost of paper, following the lead of oil. This has trebled since 1973 and replaced printing as the biggest single item of cost. Percentage breakdowns of costs for *TVTimes* have been (years ending July) can be seen in Table 18.5.

Devaluation of the pound has made a major contribution to the leap in paper prices and we must hope for more stability as the pound becomes stronger against Scandinavian currencies. The printer's bill is governed by his own costs, in particular his wage bill. There have therefore been continual and substantial increases, and these will no doubt continue.

The relationship between costs and the two sources of revenue is complex. Selling more advertising means adding extra pages and this has to be assessed against the costs of preparing and printing the pages. Selling more copies does not involve any extra preparatory costs but brings in no extra advertisement revenue. The high cost of paper frequently results in this running-on cost exceeding the additional revenue from sales. In general terms, with a cover price of 12p, revenue from extra sales equals the additional running-on cost when the issue size is sixty-four pages. On larger issues we are out of pocket. When (if ever) free from government price control, one could again aspire to fixing a

	1970	1972	1974	1976
Printing	48.4	51.9	46.5	41.5
Paper	30.7	30.9	38.9	42.5
Carriage	2.1	2.1	2.2	3.0
All other	18.8	15.1	12.4	13.0
	100.0	100.0	100.0	100.0

Table 18.5 TVTimes' costs, 1970-76

cover price which would make running-on always profitable. But if that were to mean a price above what the market would bear, then sales, and consequently advertisement, revenue would be lost. While the most profitable circulation might be thought of as the lowest figure at which advertisements are not lost or rates have to be lowered, there are long-term considerations as well as short.

As for the economies of adding pages, with a print order of 3.5 million the cost of eight extra pages in monotone amounts to more than £25000. With a basic mono rate of £4650 per page and after allowing for agency commission, more than six of the eight pages would need to be advertisement pages simply to cover the cost. Eight extra pages in full colour to meet advertisers' demands is a more profitable proposition, but not greatly so.

The tight schedule is another cost factor. Given more time, it would be possible to print on three machines instead of five. And, of course, the need to produce thirteen editions affects editorial, production, distribution and advertising alike. Edition changes mean that a ninety-six-page issue using a double colour bank requires no fewer than 101 cylinders, and a third colour bank is available and used when the demand for colour necessitates it, raising the number of cylinders to 110. Separate colour for each edition is possible, but cost—at £2000 or more per page change—confines colour changes to combinations of editions (grouped according to the machines used).

Conclusion

TVTimes can be and has been very profitable, but in relation to current costs, cover price and advertisement rates are both unduly low. Price legislation effectively prevents a prudent pricing policy based on an estimate of impending rises in costs. Only when these have actually been incurred can an application for an increase in cover price or advertisement rates be submitted. And while one is picking one's way through the Price Commission's obstacle course, a handsome weekly surplus can all too easily become a devastating weekly deficit. Last year's Christmas number of *TVTimes,* for example, must have been the biggest-selling issue of any magazine published in Britain, or indeed Western Europe, for several years, but at the time when we had to make the necessary commitments it remained quite uncertain whether we would come out with a sizeable profit or an equally sizeable loss.

Small may be beautiful, but large is more exciting.

19 Small is beautiful but...

PETER FINCH

Marketing Director, British European Associated
Publishers Limited

Peter Finch is Marketing Director of British European
Associated Publishers Limited. After agency training with
OBM, he joined The Sunday Times in 1962 as marketing
support man for the new Colour Magazine. He was
marketing supervisor for the launches of Family Circle in
1964, Living in 1967, YOU Magazine (Oops!) in 1971, and
for the successful resuscitation as a monthly of the moribund
weekly, Illustrated London News. In 1973 he joined his ex-
Thomson chief, Geoffrey Perry, and they launched Home &
Freezer Digest a year later. His premature grey hairs are all
due, he says, to the extreme reluctance of agency media
planners to support new publications.

When a small publisher breaks into the big time, observers
look for the special ingredient of success. So naturally, *Home*
& Freezer Digest has come under the microscope. Some of
the alleged success factors relate specifically to the freezer
market. Others could in theory be of general application. In
this article we look at the significance of three factors which

make *Home & Freezer Digest* a little different from its competitors. They are:

1. The digest format.
2. The small number of staff in the publishing company.
3. Distribution through food outlets as well as the legitimate news trade.

Small is beautiful. Or is it?

When BEAP launched a women's magazine in the 7 × 5 ins. digest format, our competitors were sceptical. At the same time they were nervous that we might just have stumbled on the crock of gold for which they had long searched in vain. Printers suddenly had enquiries fluttering through their letterboxes asking for quotes on similar specifications. However, nothing new has emerged in this size. The big boys have apparently satisfied themselves that BEAP have not found the jackpot end of the rainbow. And, of course, they are right.

Agencies also suspected that they were being bowled a fast ball—if not actually an illegal one. They calculated that a 7 × 5 ins. magazine yields thirty-five square inches per page, and that an 11 × 8 ins. magazine yields eighty-nine square inches. Costs of production, they reckoned, vary *pro rata* to printed surface area. Yet here were these people from BEAP trying to charge us the same cost per thousand for their mini page that other publishers charge for the normal page. Not quite cricket, old man.

I did not take kindly to the hint of moral indignation. Most media people are ignorant of magazine economics, just as I am ignorant of agency economics. So two simple tabulations (Table 19.1 and Table 19.2) put things into perspective. *Home & Freezer Digest's* page is less than half the size of *Ideal Home's,* but its cost/000 is eighty-nine per cent of *Ideal Home's.* Yet when everything is taken into account, *Ideal*

Table 19.1

	Colour page	Adult readers (000's)*	Cost per colour page per 1000 adults
Ideal Home	£1,450	2,598	£0.56
Home & Freezer Digest	£1,000	1,987	£0.50

*JICNARS July 1976 to June 1977

Table 19.2

	Ideal Home	*Home & Freezer Digest*
Av. ABC July 1976 to June 1977	179,410	357,949
Page size (square inches)	89.6	37.2
September issue size (pages)	172	104
September ad. volume (pages)	79	41.5
Gross ad. revenue for issue	£105,000*	£35,000
Gross ad. revenue per ad. page	£1,329	£858
Gross ad. revenue per mag. page	£610.5	£342.3
Gross ad. revenue per mag. page per 1,000 copies ABC	£3.40	£0.956
Gross ad. revenue per sq. inch of magazine page per 1000 copies ABC	3.79p	2.57p

*BEAP Estimate based on monitoring the issue

Home's advertising take per square inch of magazine page is nearly fifty per cent more than *Home & Freezer Digest's*. So who is profiteering?

The lesson is that the media planner should stick to his last. As a market-oriented man (hopefully), he should ask himself whether a publisher's advertisement rates represent a competitive buy for his client. The publisher's revenues are really none of his business, and in any case it is unlikely that he will ever be able to see enough of the cost side of the picture to make economic judgments, let alone moral strictures.

Format relates primarily to the whole style and philosophy of a magazine. It is a case of horses for courses.

Back in 1973 BEAP had a brief flirtation with *Over 21* and its dynamic creator, Audrey Slaughter. Audrey said that she had always fancied the prospects for a digest-sized woman's magazine. After all, she reasoned, the IPC weeklies are seventy-five per cent puff, and the remaining twenty-five per cent would fit comfortably into a 7 × 5 ins. page. It was a thought.

It does not follow, however, that the format of the weeklies is wasteful. If their role is to fill the aching void between breakfast and bedtime, then the more long-winded they are the better their readers like them. Similarly with the decor magazines; if the readers buy them for a vicarious glimpse of gracious living, then the bigger the sheet of paper you print them on, the more imposing the marble halls will appear in the eye of the beholder.

With service magazines a different set of criteria apply. Women buy them for information. They want facts, not flannel. They do not want a hundred words where fifty will do. They do not want a long word where a short one will do. There are some women—mainly working wives—who actually are busy (as opposed to merely thinking they are busy), and they appreciate a taut, economic use of language.

The mood of the market-place is also important. BEAP launched *Home & Freezer Digest* in 1974—the year when the FT Index fell from 339 to 150. Inflation was raging, and the

white-collar classes (that is you and I) were bearing the brunt.
People were buying freezers in the hope of saving money.
Bulk buying; batch baking; grow your own; buy now, eat
later—these were the themes the new magazine would take
up. It was back to the protestant ethic—Thriftiness is next to
Godliness.

A magazine based on this philosophy could hardly appear
as an expansive, high cover-price glossy. So *Home & Freezer
Digest* had to look inexpensive and it had to be inexpensive.
The digest format obviously provided production economies,
and it seemed, at the same time, an appropriate vehicle for
the editorial approach.

When agencies assess the digest format they are trapped by
their own semantics. Because they employ space-buyers they
seem to think their job is to buy space. It is not. Their job is
to buy opportunities in a channel of communication.

When a TV campaign is on the stocks, nobody concerns
himself with the size of screen in the viewers home. I can't
remember seeing statistics which tell me what per cent of
Southern TV viewers have twenty-two-inch sets or what the
index is for seventeen-inch screens in Central Scotland.

Media planners and creative staff do concern themselves
with the length of spot. 'Can we get the message across in
fifteen seconds, or do we need thirty?' This is a much more
relevant question. Essentially it boils down to this: 'Can we
communicate the advertiser's message effectively within this
communications opportunity?'.

Gallup Noting & Reading scores suggest that the average
full-page advertisement in digest format communicates as
well—no better, no worse—than the average full-page
advertisement in A4 format. The media planner should,
therefore, concern himself with whether a particular creative
treatment can actually be contained in a particular space.
However, time and tide wait for no man, and the creative
department is always late. So nine times out of ten the
planner prepares his schedule without any clear idea of what
the advertisement will look like.

The media proprietor also has a problem with creative

people. They like to see their advertisements in big spaces, and their gut reactions tend to be anti-digest, but since they rarely come face-to-face with media salesmen, they do not have to justify themselves.

Media selling is really a confidence business. For the planner faced with new publications, it is more important to avoid losers than to back winners. To make his stance respectable, the planner invents a series of objections to any publication whose future he regards as uncertain. He is like the doll with a weighted base. You can floor him a dozen times, and he still comes up again with the same old grin on his face. No matter how many objections you destroy, he will find some more.

The salesman's consolation is that, once a publication is established and confidence built up, the planner's objections vanish. The objections were there to hide the planner's fears; when the fear dissolves, the objections melt like morning mists under a warm sun.

This is true of all new launches. In the case of a digest magazine, format provides the planner with one more barrier to erect, and is an additional hazard on the perilous road to profitability.

The second advantage ascribed to *Home & Freezer Digest* is the small number of staff employed to produce the magazine. It is true that we are a small company, and I believe that it does give us some advantages. However, I have seen no evidence to suggest that the ratio of overheads to turnover is markedly different in the small company from what it is among the monoliths. The advantages of the small publisher are all to do with communications and morale.

Decision making is quicker in the small company. There are fewer egos to be massaged and no empires to be built and defended. When I floated the idea of a JICNARS-based rate guarantee on *Family Circle* some years ago, it took weeks of lobbying and a knock-down-and-drag-out in the boardroom before it was adopted. With *Home & Freezer Digest* a similar move was agreed and implemented in forty-eight hours.

More people see more of the picture in the small publishing

house. We used to sort our mail in reception. The size of the Monday morning mountain was a good indicator of the success of our competitions and reader offers, and every member of staff had to climb over it on the way to his desk.

I remember having a problem at Leo Burnett over Cadbury's Chocolate Buttons. They wouldn't believe that *Home & Freezer Digest* held any interest for mothers of young children. I made no impression whatsoever until I emptied on the floor of Bryan Labette's office a mail sack containing several thousand entries for a baby competition. (He stopped me before I up-ended the other three sacks.) There was nothing very clever about that tactic, but I suspect the representatives at IPC would not know where to look for the mail-room, and probably would not be allowed in if they found it.

The advantages of the small publisher are that you have a close-knit team, all committed exclusively to one title. If it succeeds, they succeed. If it fails, they are back on the breadline.

The big publisher has advantages of a different kind. He can draft in an army of auxiliaries from his other publications to sell a new title. He can offer deals which fill the advertisement pages of his new title at the expense of discounts off his mainliners. This way he can fill the first issue when not a genuine penny has been committed to it. This is very reassuring for the planner; if the publication fails, he will not be the only man with egg on his face—and in any case he could reasonably claim that the experiment has cost the client nothing.

Overall, I feel the balance of advantage still lies with the big fish rather than the minnows. The critical factor is cash. Consumer magazines eat up a lot of it before they get established, and you must have some stable bread-winners to provide the cash flow. Small companies do not have that luxury, and bankers are not keen to lend on such speculative ventures.

BEAP is a small company, but seventy-six per cent of the shares are owned by VNU, Holland's equivalent of IPC.

Small is beautiful, but it is nice to have a big sugar-daddy beside you.

Could a big publisher organise himself in such a way as to reproduce the motivation and team-spirit of the small company? I suppose it is conceivable that IPC could run its sixty-nine consumer titles as sixty-nine separate businesses, but I doubt whether it will ever happen. The single publication approach requires for each title a publisher—an entrepreneur with flair and expertise in the major functions of publishing. These people do not grow on trees. If a man starts in advertisement sales, he rarely has the opportunity (or the desire) to switch his career successively into editorial, circulation and production. So it seems likely that the giants will go on being giants, and the small companies, if they prosper, will become giants in their turn. The success of the small company approach contains the seed of its own destruction.

A third distinctive feature of *Home & Freezer Digest* is its distribution. Most magazines are sold exclusively through the news trade. *Family Circle* and *Living* are sold exclusively via the food trade. *Home & Freezer Digest* sells principally through the news trade, but with the approval of the NFRN (National Federation of Retail Newsagents), also sells through a limited number of freezer centres and other major frozen food retailers.

Some of our competitors look enviously at this dual distribution. The grass is always greener on the other side of the fence.

There is one reason why freezer centres provide a special benefit for *Home & Freezer Digest.* Since 1974 freezer ownership has expanded by four per cent per annum, and growth seems likely to continue at this rate for some years. Around 800000 housewives each year are acquiring a freezer for the first time. Most of them will visit a freezer centre, and will see *Home & Freezer Digest* in a location where it does not have to compete for display space with a hundred other titles. That is the benefit, and we think it outweighs the disadvantages, which are several.

First, the food trade is a much more expensive channel. The UK news trade is not a brilliant sales machine, but as a distributive network it is quick, reliable and highly cost-effective. BEAP make 350 wholesale deliveries to service 25000 newsagents; we make 400 deliveries to service 400 frozen food retailers. The retail drops are much smaller, so that the delivery cost per copy is significantly higher.

Second, the staff of the food outlets are not accustomed to handling magazines, which must be put on and taken off sale on specific dates, with unsolds returned for credit. The result is that each outlet has to be visited each month by a merchandiser—another cost burden.

Third, food stores need special fitments to stock magazines. That is money. Then the racks have to be installed. That is more money.

Fourth, notwithstanding the arrangements BEAP made with the NFRN, some newsagents still are irritated by the sight of magazines in food stores. At one stage the W.H. Smith shop in Romford was selling over 1000 copies of *Home & Freezer Digest*. The manager was ecstatic: apart from the TV papers, he was not accustomed to ordering magazines by the thousand. It then happened that we supplied Sainsburys in the same shopping precinct. The W.H. Smith manager responded by cutting his order to such an extent that our combined sales through W.H. Smith and Sainsbury were less than fifty per cent of our original sale. Crazy, maybe, but it happened. It illustrates the potential for aggro in dual distribution.

We hear repeated rumours that IPC are going to attempt a supermarket magazine, and we hear threats from the news wholesalers of what will happen if they do. There should be quite a fireworks display if it ever happens. I think it will not happen.

There is one critical point about magazine sales through supermarkets: you need display at the checkout. In the USA most supermarkets have a magazine rack, carrying a hundred or so titles. They also have magazines at the checkout—usually the big four—*Family Circle, Woman's*

Day, Reader's Digest and *TV Guide. Family Circle's* experience was that their sales dropped by ninety per cent if they were moved from the checkout to the general magazine rack. Standbrook have had the same experience in this country. It is not enough to be in supermarkets; you have got to have that semi-solus display at the checkout.

Family Circle and *Living* had a tough time getting to the checkout and their futures depend on staying there. Supermarket operators like uncluttered checkouts and newcomers will find it even harder work to get in. And it will be expensive. Who knows better than Tesco how to screw the last ha'penny out of a supplier?

It may well be that, within a few years, most supermarkets will have a magazine and paperback section. This may make life difficult for neighbouring newsagents, but it will not radically alter the prospects for publishers.

In my opinion the success of *Home & Freezer Digest* cannot be attributed either to its format, or to its method of distribution, or to the small company approach to publishing. Maybe we should look not at the distinguishing features of individual successes but at what they have in common. As a marketing man it hurts me to admit it, but the key factor is the publisher who finds an editor with the flair to produce a magazine that customers want to buy.

Where does the small publisher find this undiscovered paragon? The odds are she is already toiling away in the clutches of one of the wicked giants, the blue-print for a best-seller hidden away in her bottom drawer. She is waiting for a daring, handsome entrepreneur to liberate her, and power her brainchild to the top of the ABC charts. All you need is a cheque for a million pounds and she is yours.

20   Guess who's coming to launch?

BRIAN BRAITHWAITE

Publisher, Cosmopolitan

Brian Braithwaite is the Publisher of Cosmopolitan. He has also been Publisher of Harpers Bazaar and Vanity Fair and was the Publisher responsible for the merger of Harpers and Queen. He was the Advertisement Director of Queen when owned by Jocelyn Stevens. He helped to launch New Scientist and New Society and has also worked for Associated Newspapers and Hulton Press.

After the big shake-out of the fifties and the early sixties, when the end of paper rationing and the advent of commercial TV slaughtered many of the famous old titles of the women's magazine business, there came a bright optimistic period of new women's magazines—a sort of Launchtime O'Booze. Most of these titles were aimed at the younger end of the market and most of the titles are extant. There were, however, some notable backsliders, like *Nova* and *Flair, Fashion* and *Woman's Mirror.*

In a hugely volatile business like women's magazines there is inevitably a lot of movement and a lot of change. But as the sheer capital costs of launching a new magazine have grown, so the advent of new launches had receded. The most sensationally successful new woman's magazine launched has to be *Cosmopolitan* in March 1972. The first year's advertising campaigns, mostly on television and national newspapers, totalled about £200000. As the cost of television has doubled in the past five years it would seem that the sum of money needed to launch a major new woman's magazine in 1978 would be about £400000. And the launch of *Cosmopolitan* was attended by the most carefully constructed PR campaign which is still talked about today by the cognoscenti. No launch since *Cosmopolitan* has been able to emulate even a tenth of the excitement or impact of that immeasurable free publicity.

Since the beginning of the seventies the general picture has changed, the factors of which make a look into the early eighties rather fascinating. IPC has now built itself into a conglomerate, full of mandarins, and the old autonomous companies like Newnes, Fleetway and Odhams are no more. Because of their dominance of the women's magazine market (about twenty-eight per cent of the titles) a sudden IPC success with a new launch in the market would probably give them a painful crack in their own backside as they inflicted damage on, or even killed, one of their own titles. Fortunately or unfortunately, as the case may be, they have so far not created a new magazine vibrant enough to cause this self-inflicted wound. But the danger is nevertheless there. Another factor is that some of the young magazines are getting on a bit. There is an arthritic twinge here, a threatened prolapse there. The new generation of young women will want new magazines, not the ones their big sisters have been reading, let alone their mothers. So some of the older titles will be led to the abattoir and new ones will be needed to replace them.

And yet another factor is the absence, because of failures or lack of money, of the new publishing companies and the new entrepreneurs. A Tom Eyton, able to start *Slimming Magazine* almost as a cottage industry and to see it grow to its present success, is very much the exception to the rule. Perhaps we should mourn the passing of *Prima*—not because i: had the slightest merit as a publication (indeed it was so feeble it is surprising that it lasted the year that it did) but because an outside company, the BSR record turntable firm, invested in the magazine and if it had been successful presumably would have been encouraged to expand. Instead, they have scuttled back, quite understandably, to the calmer waters of the turntable business.

One would like to think that in garrets at the moment are young creative dreamers hatching up really new ideas for women's magazines and they will shortly emerge, blinking in the daylight, with their dummies in one hand and their bankrolls in the other. The truth is different. Their ideas will have to be taken to one of the big companies who would be able to subsidise the massive consumer and trade publicity, as well as the initial launch costs, and perhaps even bear a substantial early issue loss even if the magazine eventually becomes successful and profit-making.

The fourth factor which has contributed to the launch gloom has to be the boring old story of inflationary costs. Paper and print have increased about two-and-a-quarter times since 1972 and the cost rises of staff, offices and all the usual business accoutrements are familiar to all of us. But paper and print are the publisher's meat and drink and the savage increases of the past five years help to ensure that a launch failure of a magazine aiming at the 300000 circulation level can be a very painful lesson indeed.

So where will the market move in the next five years? There will probably be a development of the franchised magazine. This is when a publisher in one country sells a publisher in another country the franchise rights of his editorial. The new publisher adapts it for his own market and pays a cover price and advertising royalty to the franchiser. It can be most profitable for both parties. The Hearst Corporation in New York has been developing the idea successfully with their overseas edition of *Cosmopolitan*—there are now fourteen overseas editions on a franchise. *Parents* magazine is a UK franchise of the German *Eltern* and there are other franchisees of this title throughout the world. The idea is open to limitless development and has the twin advantages of a ready-proved magazine and the use of reams of back numbers and smaller editorial staffs.

One also has to keep a weather-eye open for the continental publishers who are eyeing our market with interest. The great Dutch publishers VNU have already made their initial incursion here with the formation of British European Publishers and their launch of *Home & Freezer Digest* and *Knitting and Craft Digest.* Other continentals, notably the Germans, are very possible publishers in this country.

We must avoid any confusion of a launch with a relaunch. Relaunches do not work. It is difficult, if not impossible, to think of a successful relaunch in the women's magazine market. There have been mergers (and *Harpers & Queen* is probably the outstanding example of a real merger) but usually a merger is simply the closure of one title into another. Relaunches are a sort of cosmetic, desperate attempt at rejuvenation that will inevitably fail and if the readers are deserting your magazine you are not going to attract new ones (and try to keep the old ones) by such sledge-hammer tactics. Better to close your magazine and launch a new one for the new readers you are after—if you can afford a launch.

There will be more deaths as this decade draws to a close. Whatever happens in the woman's weekly market one cannot see a *new* weekly being launched by anybody. The last three attempts, *Eve, Candida* and *First Lady,* died in very early infancy. Indeed, the last-named one actually died in the womb. The young titles, as already mentioned, are in for some severe shuffling of the pack and quite a few other monthlies must be getting a long hard look at their bottom lines. At the end of the day, every magazine has a positive life cycle. Sometimes the cycle is very short and sometimes the magazine seems immortal. But the successful ones are just enjoying a longer life cycle and in the fullness of time they will be led to the guillotine or be merged into a rival title. Of all the hundred or so titles extant today in the woman's magazine market, only two date back to 1910/1911 and two from 1919. As costs keep trundling upwards, and cover prices continue to climb, the path will get harder and the toll will be more severe. This will mean, of course, that the launches will have to take place to replenish the stocks of the late-lamented titles.

We perhaps all agree that the day of the general magazine, and that includes the general woman's magazine, is over. Specialisation is still the name of the game but this too has its dangers. Any circulation under 150000 is not generally viable or particularly attractive as a publishing investment. Advertisers in women's magazines have too much choice of media to be able to afford to be altruistic towards over-specialised titles. This is not to say that the glossies will not continue to prosper (but with ever higher cover prices) or a magazine like *The Lady* with its own special niche of all those Norfolk sea-side cottages and Norland nannies. The specialisation will come successfully to those magazines which can isolate a large and positive segment of the women's market to make a viable publishing proposition and offer certain advertisers the market segment they require. *Cosmopolitan* has done this, as have *Home & Freezer Digest* and *Slimming*. In the USA there is a highly successful title called *Essence* which is aimed at black women. This is the perfect example of specialisation to a positive and sizeable market. The market is obviously limited but it is entirely relevant that there should be such a magazine. Its circulation in 1976 reached 500000 and it enjoyed an advertisement revenue of nearly $4 million.

The way ahead is not going to be easy for the launcher. Having assembled the sort of money needed to create the demand it is then necessary to come forward with a concept that is going to be relevant to its intended audience. There has to be editorial integrity, a *raison d'être* and a demand which is not being satisfied elsewhere. There are going to be new editorial styles needed as well as physical and technical changes. The challenge is great but the rewards for the successful will be satisfying.

There *will* be new launches. The money *will* be found and even new entrepreneurs *will* appear from somewhere. Maybe some eccentric millionaires are waiting round the corner looking for investment possibilities, maybe record turntable companies will not be too discouraged and will diversify into magazine publishing. Maybe the biggest conglomerate will find ways of decentralising and find more excitement and real internecine competition.

Women's magazines are too potent a force not to keep developing and changing with the times. They will continue to make a maximum contribution to the media mix.

21   Specialist magazines

DAVID ARCULUS
*Deputy Managing Director, EMAP National Publications
Limited*

*David Arculus left Oxford University in 1968. After a period
as a BBC Producer he took a postgraduate MSc in
Economics and then joined EMAP in 1972. He is currently
Deputy Managing Director of Peterborough-based EMAP
National Publications Ltd. EMAP is involved in provincial
newspapers including two evenings, specialist magazines of
which they publish fifteen, printing and retailing.*

The specialist magazine market is at present highly
competitive, with a number of established publishers
competing hard within the market and with peripheral
competition from television, radio, books, part-works and
newspapers. To put it in the context of the consumer
magazine market as a whole, I shall define specialist magazines
as covering titles devoted to specific leisure or hobby
activities — sailing, motoring, gardening, aero-modelling,
etc., but not magazines aimed at mass consumer markets i.e.
women's magazines, men's magazines or comics. Because of
their specialised nature specialist titles tend to have lower
circulations than general magazines. Circulations range from

10000 up to about 200000. In the main the trend is towards smaller circulations; coupled with this is a tendency towards market segmentation as new publications enter to cater for particular sub-specialisations.

It is a market which changes rapidly and where success goes to those with the best ideas, the ability to predict new interests, and the ability to exploit them. It also is much easier to launch a specialist magazine than, say, a mass circulation women's magazine and so, wherever one publication carves out a success for itself, others spring up. 'Wherever there is one successful publication there is room for another' is a maxim which one often hears at gatherings of magazine publishers.

Profits and profit/turnover ratios tend to fall somewhere between those of the highly profitable provincial press and those of the rather unprofitable national newspapers. Return on capital can be quite high; after all, in the ultimate all one needs is a good idea, some office furniture, and a friendly printer willing to give credit until the money starts coming in.

The economics of the specialist press have to be considered against this background of strong competition, far removed from the monopoly positions of much of the regional press, or the bottomless pocket with which many of the proprietors of the national press are apparently blessed.

The specialist press as a whole depends fairly evenly on circulation and advertising revenues. In the last few years circulation had tended to become more important, principally because cover prices have risen faster than advertisement rates. As far as costs are concerned the most important elements are production and paper costs. Paper costs have risen very rapidly this decade, but fortunately for the publisher this has been partly balanced by print costs, which have not increased nearly so fast. I shall look briefly at paper and production costs and then go on to discuss in somewhat more detail the economics of specialist magazine publishing.

Paper

Expenditure on paper is the most important ingredient in the publisher's costs. This unfortunately is probably the area over which he has least control. The main factor affecting the price appears to be the state of the world economy. Paper consumption and economic growth go hand in hand—not, as you might think, a defence of the state bureaucracies which dominate the industrial nations, but rather a reflection of the increased paging which results from higher advertising in a growing economy. The key to it all is the United States economy. When it grows rapidly as in 1972-3 there is a great shortage of paper, and prices are bid up. When it is relatively stagnant, as now, prices are relatively stable.

British magazine and newspaper publishers had five very bad years with spiralling paper costs due to: (a) economic growth in the United States, followed by (b) a steady depreciation in the rate of sterling relative to the Scandinavians and the Canadians—the main paper suppliers.

This year things are much better. The US economy is in the doldrums; hence demand is quite slack, and the Scandinavians have recently devalued their currency relative to sterling. Even so, publishers are still on the look out for savings in paper costs and most are looking hard at either dropping grammage, reducing paper quality or reducing wastage at the print stage. Being by far the biggest expenditure of the publisher, the price of paper has the most direct influence on both cover prices and advertisement rates.

Production

The rapid rises in paper prices have been partly nullified by the incredibly fortunate situation which publishers have found themselves in as far as buying print is concerned. Printers have been crying out for work and to a surprising

extent magazine publishers have been able to dictate the price
that they will pay. What are the reasons for this? The tax and
depreciation laws must bear a large share of the credit. Free
depreciation, investment grants, regional policy and the like
have helped to encourage investment in extra press capacity.
Once plant is installed it is very difficult to justify closing or
not using it, and so prices have tended to reflect marginal
costs rather than full costs. The consequences have been
cheap print coupled with very low profits for printers. Several
major printers are in loss situations and others are able to
continue to compete through such schemes as the Temporary
Employment Premium.

Much has been written about inefficiencies in the print
industry. This may be true in Fleet Street, as indeed in the
provincial newspaper industry, but I would argue that as far
as magazine printers are concerned these competitive forces
have made firms much more efficient than their counterparts
in other segments. Of course you do not get anything for
nothing, and it is arguable that this very price competitiveness
may have led to a fall in the final quality of the printed
product.

In my own company, EMAP (East Midland Allied Press
Ltd), we have been especially fortunate in having a great part
of our print produced internally. Besides newspaper printing
facilities, we have facilities for full colour pre-print for our
three specialist newspapers, *Angling Times, Garden News*
and *Motor Cycle News,* plus a magazine press. The great
advantage of this has been that we have guaranteed high
quality print facilities right on our doorstep. The appearance
of our publications has benefited accordingly and with it their
appeal to advertisers and readers.

This advantage is currently being further exploited by the
installation of a Koenig and Bauer 'Commander' magazine
press capable of producing high quality colour magazines at
speeds approaching 50000 per hour. The strong points of this
press will be high quality colour, plus low wastage and the
ability to produce quality results on relatively cheap paper.

Magazine economics

The market for specialist magazines is fiercely competitive, IPC is of course the market leader dominating the consumer and leisure markets. But it has several smaller companies offering it competition in particular segments. In this category would come companies such as Argus, Link House, National Magazine, Haymarket and EMAP, to name but a few.

In many ways this competition is healthy; it means that no one company has the monopoly in a particular market and it ensures that cover prices and advertisement rates are kept competitive—some would argue too competitive. For instance, as Harry Henry demonstrated in Chapter 1, between 1971-6 the average increase in media rates on all consumer magazines was 75 per cent. During that same period inflation ran at 96 per cent, and the price of paper rose by 180 per cent. Cover prices rose 114 per cent in the comparable period— faster than the inflation rate but not by as much as the increase in paper costs.

These figures, of course, cover a multitude of different situations. The average circulation of consumer magazines has fallen over the period quoted so bearing in mind the cost per thousand readers the imbalance in advertisement rates has not been quite so marked.

However there is little doubt that advertisement rates have, in real terms, declined and that the brunt of the increases in paper costs have been borne by the consumer. What are the reasons for this? The first is that in the early 1970s there was very little resistance to cover price increases. Perhaps we were all getting wealthier, perhaps we were all confused by the new money; whatever the reason it became easy to pass cost increases straight on to the consumer. In the long run this may be the reason or part-reason why circulations are declining, but in the short run the attractions of cover price rises were quite compelling. So publishers pushed their cover prices up.

Advertisement rates by contrast have lagged behind. One reason for this has been that in a time of rising inflation there has been a temptation to pass on such costs as were allowable under the price control legislation as quickly as possible. The effect of a ten per cent change on the cover price is much more immediate than ten per cent on the advertisement rates where series arrangements, gentleman's agreements, undercutting by the opposition, early copy deadlines and the like, tend to delay implementation of the rate increase.

Another reason has been that advertisers and agencies have treated any rate increase as a personal betrayal, whilst the ordinary consumer has not been quite so vociferous. Despite the tremendous increase in paper prices and the inability to pass the increases on to advertisers, publishers have survived—partly through rising cover prices, partly through reductions in paper weight, partly through tightening advertising to editorial ratios. That this situation must change seems undeniable. People have less money to spend, circulations are declining.

In the meantime there are some quite outstanding bargains for advertisers in the specialist press. *Practical Gardening,* for instance, will deliver 1.6 million readers for a page rate of £275. *Practical Photography* will deliver just over 1 million readers for a page rate of £230 (TGI).

Given figures like this, it seems surprising that there is still relatively little general consumer advertising in the specialist press. No one would suggest that specialist publications should be the prime medium for promoting general consumer goods, but agencies do seem to have been slow in realising the extra coverage that can be added to schedules by a very small investment in specialist media. There is the added advantage of the impact and unexpectedness of a general consumer advertisement in a specialist publication.

Here may lie one solution—given an expansion in volume it may be possible to maintain advertisement rates somewhere near their present low figures. If this is what the agency world wants the solution lies in its own hands.

Cover prices versus advertisement rates

The question is often asked as to whether advertising subsidises the magazine buyers or whether the buyer subsidises the advertiser. Certainly without advertising, or with very little advertising, cover prices would need to be much higher, so to that extent advertising does subsidise the consumer—although as we have seen not by nearly as much as it did at the start of the decade. Also in most situations the subsidy is strictly limited to the extent that the publisher would expect the extra revenue from additional sales to cover the extra production costs in obtaining those sales. By the same token he would expect extra advertisement revenue to cover the cost of adding extra pages to accommodate that revenue. So whatever pricing structure publishers adopt they normally expect the marginal sales revenue to cover marginal production costs.

There are exceptions to this rule: mass circulation titles with falling circulations sometimes need to subsidise extra readers to justify their advertisement rates, but such instances are rare.

Over the last few years there have been two main beneficiaries from rising cover prices, the advertisers—for rates have not increased as fast as they might, and the retailers—who tend to work on a fixed percentage of the cover price.

The future

Circulations are declining in the specialist press. Cover price increases must slow down. If the present diversity of titles is to continue it can only be because of an increase in advertisement revenue—either through volume or rate increases or both. However there are some hopeful signs. The amount of time devoted to specialist leisure activities by the average citizen is increasing, partly because of shorter working weeks, partly because of longer holidays, partly because of better education. When people spend time on things they usually have to spend money as well, and where there is money spent there are advertisers. If this advertising support does materialise titles can survive and indeed new ones can be launched. For specialist publishers the theory of survival of the fittest seems particularly appropriate. However, many of them face the future with hope and with some degree of confidence.

PART VI

Trade and technical magazines

22 The economics of the trade and technical press

HAROLD LIND

Harold Lind studied philosophy at Oxford and remained there to teach formal logic, later switching to economics. He worked among other places at the National Institute of Economic and Social Research. From 1968 to 1977 he was Director of Research at the Advertising Association. He is now Head of Information Services at AGB Research Ltd.

He is author of a number of books and articles including Attitudes in British Industry, Regional Policy in Britain and the EEC, Public Attitudes to Advertising, and Economic Aspects of Advertising.

'Small earthquake in Chile, Not many dead' is usually regarded as the dullest headline of all time. If so, for most people, 'The Economics of the Trade and Technical Press' must run it a close second. Obviously I am not in sympathy with the explosion of indifference which overwhelms commentators on the media when they come to discuss trade and technical press, otherwise I would not be writing this chapter. But I believe that an understanding of the reasons for the lack of impact of the apparently quite impressive statistics of the trade and technical press will greatly help us in discovering the true but usually ignored economic springs which move this media sector.

The bare bones of the economic background to the trade and technical press can be given quickly, and at first sight provide little clue to the lack of interest generated by this medium. In terms of advertising revenue (on Advertising Association definitions) the trade and technical press received £103m in 1976, which makes it a slightly bigger advertising medium than the consumer magazines' sector (£92m) and approximately five times bigger than radio— a sector which at the moment is oozing with glamour and attracting immense interest. As with most press sectors, trade and technical magazines do not receive all their revenue from advertising, many (although not all) also have a cover price, and this increases the total revenue coming to the sector. According to the Central Statistical Office Business Monitor on Newspapers and Periodicals (which, readers should be warned, is by no means always a completely reliable source of data in this area) approximately three-fifths of net revenue in the trade and technical sector comes from advertising, the remainder from the cover price. The Business Monitor figures for these two categories in 1976 are £86m and £63m respectively. Those who understand advertising statistics will appreciate that the Business Monitor's net revenue figures for advertising are not directly comparable with the gross figures produced by the Advertising Association. Those who are still better acquainted with the figures will appreciate that the Business Monitor figures are significantly lower than they ought to be if the difference was merely due to agency commission, as it should be. Fortunately it will make relatively little difference for our purposes whether we accept the total revenue figure as the £149m given by the Business Monitor, or take a figure between £10m and £30m higher which would be implied by the AA definitions.

	Amount Spent £m	Proportion of Total %
1960	31	9.6
64	37	8.9
68	46	9.1
72	61	8.6
73	73	8.4
74	80	8.9
75	86	8.9
76	103	8.7

Source: Advertising Association

Table 22.1 Advertising in the trade and technical press

	Trade & Technical	Magazines & Periodicals	Radio	TV
1960	9.6	12.4	0.3	22.3
64	8.9	11.1	0.5	24.5
68	9.1	9.9	0.2	25.6
72	8.6	8.5	0.1	24.9
73	8.4	8.2	0.2	24.0
74	8.9	7.9	0.7	22.6
75	8.9	8.2	1.1	24.4
76	8.7	7.7	1.8	25.1

Source: Advertising Association

Table 22.2 Various media as a proportion of advertising expenditure

In 1976 the trade and technical press accounted for 8.7 per cent of all media advertising expenditure. In itself this figure does not mean very much, but Table 22.2 shows an interesting contrast between the trade and technical press and other media, and perhaps one which begins to explain the lack of interest shown in this area. Its relative stability as a proportion of total advertising between 1960 and 1976 is in strong contrast to, for instance the magazine and periodical sector, whose share has fallen heavily over the period, and to radio and directories whose share has risen. But of equally great interest is the relative smallness of the year to year fluctuations. Television, for instance, has not markedly altered its long-term proportion of advertising expenditure over the last fifteen years, but it is susceptible to very considerable year to year swings, which give writers on the media the opportunity of displaying their lack of perspective with stories on the imminent demise of commercial television or the forthcoming millenium. The general year to year stability of the trade and technical press as a whole does not generate this kind of comment, and therefore helps to reduce interest in the medium. However, since from an economic point of view relative stability is safer and more efficient than wild economic swings, those who are involved in the trade and technical sector may well bear this type of indifference with considerable fortitude.

So far my description of the economics of the trade and technical press has had a distinctly negative quality. We know that it is not suspectible to violent swings, and is not markedly gaining or losing in advertising terms, but we do not yet know what sort of medium it is. An analogy is helpful here. Television is a medium largely aimed at the mass consumer, and vulnerable to economic trends which affect firms' propensity to sell competitively. Similarly regional newspapers are heavily dependent on classified advertising, particularly for recruitment, and are therefore vulnerable if the job market turns down, making job advertisements less necessary. Can we give a similar thumb nail sketch of the economic forces governing the wellbeings of the trade and technical sector? I used to believe that we could, but I was wrong. However this mistake turned out to be highly educative for me, and I hope may prove so for others.

Every student of media statistics is aware that most broad media categories tend to include, more or less by default, a number of titles which have little in common with the main bulk of the category. This is obviously the case with the trade and technical press, as defined either by the Advertising Association or the Business Monitor, for instance the so-called 'professional press' which can cover anything from school magazines to the *Lancet*. The one thing this variegated collection of journals has in common is that all its members are markedly different from one's normal conceptions of trade or business magazines.

However, when discussing the economics of the trade press, this is a known and relatively minor nuisance. I believed for a number of years that it was still perfectly proper to talk about the advertising in the trade, technical and business press as being essentially industrial advertising, and therefore to regard it as being largely governed by the health of the capital goods industries. This doctrine sounded plausible, and proved extremely useful when I was preparing theoretical models of trade cycle effects, to act as a basis for an econometric forecast of advertising expenditures. It is a well known fact that the capital goods industries prosper and decline at different points in the trade cycle to the consumer goods industries, and I had every expectation that these differences would show up in an analysis of advertising in the trade and technical press.

Unfortunately, as so often happens with beautiful theories, this one did not work in practice. It proved possible to show relatively close relationships between almost every other form of advertising and various economic variables (i.e. correlation co-efficients of at least 0.9) but advertising in the trade and technical press showed no significant relationships with any economic variable, and certainly not with any variable related to the capital goods industries. This made a direct forecast of the trade and technical area impossible, and was therefore annoying, but it was also puzzling. The immediate temptation was to believe that the low correlations must be due to the heterogenous nature of the titles classed as 'trade and technical', but this explanation was unsatisfactory, as it always appeared implausible that titles in this area were any more disparate than those coming under 'All newspapers', or 'Consumer periodicals', both of which provided quite acceptable correlation co-efficients with several economic variables. Further econometric work strongly confirmed this assumption by showing that the advertising expenditures in trade journals were not randomly distributed, even though they did not move directly with any of the economic trade cycle variables.

As is so often the case, the answer to the mystery of why advertising in the trade and technical press did not appear to be related to any economic variable, is in fact shatteringly obvious, and any reader who knows much about the trade and technical press should happily be able to skip the rest of this paragraph where I explain it. The key to the riddle is simply the falsity of the assumption that the trade and technical press is specifically geared to capital goods industries. The most cursory glance at Benn's Press Directory or BRAD will show that the phrase 'trade magazine' means just that—magazines which cover every conceivable trade in the country. Why should the trade magazine of grocers, or accountants or advertising men or farmers be expected to be influenced by factors affecting the capital goods industries? It is precisely because all trades are covered under the trade and technical banner that it is difficult to find a relatively small number of economic variables which directly relate to the sector as a whole. But this fact merely emphasizes the essentially unifying factor of the trade press—that each journal exists by and for the particular industry or trade group which it is designed to serve. The economic function of the sector is clear and monolithic; the confusion arises from the very large number of spheres where this economic function takes place.

These points are emphasised in a study of the trade and technical press carried out for Benn Publications Ltd *(The Trade Press in Britain)*. This makes clear the link between trade journals and their industries, although perhaps more emphasis should have been given to the corollary, namely the distance between the sphere of interest of óne journal and another, to say nothing of the distance between most journals and what can loosely be called 'the advertising industry'. This is an important point, and one which I believe is not sufficiently recognised, even perhaps by many people on the business side of trade and technical journals. Clearly the health of 'the advertising industry' is important to advertising agencies, and in general the factors which are good for agencies are also good for media such as television, consumer magazines and the national press. But the health or otherwise of the advertising industry is likely to have virtually no impact on the health of trade and technical magazines, with the exception of those like ADMAP which are journals of the advertising industry. The economics of other trade journals is a function of the economics of their own industries, and I suspect there is still considerable scope for most journals to think more closely about these economics, both to inform their readers more effectively, but also and particularly, to improve their own business efficiency.

In his speech introducing the new study, Mr James Benn, Managing Director of Benn Publications Ltd, suggested that the study *How industry sells* should really have been sponsored years earlier by the trade press, whose need for this kind of information is greater than that of almost any other group. I agree strongly with this thought, but again feel that it could be taken a stage further; how industry in general sells is important to the trade press, but how its particular industry sells must be crucial to every trade journal individually. The immediate question is how close the trade press as a whole is to maximising its efficiency as a sales and advertising medium.

Questions of this nature are always more difficult than they look, and answers to them can at best be rough subjective judgements. My feeling is that, at least until recently, many journals in the trade press left a lot to be desired as efficient business vehicles. One could make an analogy with evening newspapers twenty years ago, which were often maintained in business without too much thought about profitability, or about the possibilities of a more thorough exploitation of their markets.

During the sixties these attitudes changed markedly, leaving rather fewer evening newspapers, but in general much more profitable ones, and ones which in general made a much

	1956	1966	1971	1976
No of T&T journals	343	656	793	639
T&T Journals in ABC	85	411	485	517
ABC T&T Circulation (000's)	1767	5791	7841	8432
Average circ. per ABC journal (000's)	20.8	14.1	16.2	16.3

Source: Benn's Press Directory and ABC

Table 22.3 Number and circulation of trade and technical
          journals

more effective effort to identify their revenue raising
possibilities.

Table 22.3 shows some figures from the Benn survey which
I find rather encouraging. It seems to me highly significant
that over the last five years the number of titles in the trade and
technical sector has declined, while average circulations have
risen. This looks to me like an area which is beginning to
become more profit conscious. If the analogy of the evening
newspapers is followed further, the next step should be a
much more thorough examination by trade journals of the
sales requirements of their particular industries.

In many areas a great deal of work needs to be done by the
managers of trade papers to get this kind of information, but
I believe that the will to achieve this is beginning to appear,
and if this is so, the means should present relatively little
difficulty. I am convinced that at present there is as much
scope for economic expansion in the trade press as there was
in evening newspapers twenty years ago, and if the
opportunity is grasped, the future of most trade journals
ought to be bright, whatever the dubious fortunes of the
advertising industry as a whole.

23 Britain's knowledge industry

GEORGE C. BOGLE

George C. Bogle, CBE, is Director, Government and Industry Affairs, Reed International Limited, Director of Reed Publishing Holdings Limited, Chairman, Advertising Standards Board of Finance Limited. He was Director, Corporate Affairs, of the International Publishing Corporation, and a member of its Board of Management for five years before taking up his present appointments.

There are five million scientists and technologists at work in the world today. By the end of the century, this figure will have risen to twenty-five million. Moreover, the productivity of each will have doubled by the increased use of computers and other aids. The greatest proportion of these scientists and technologists will be working in industry: in research, development and in manufacture, as all branches of industry continue to become increasingly science-based.

Current stages of development vary enormously country by country, but national frontiers have less and less relevance to the technological revolution going on around the world. It is no longer possible to think in terms of less than a world market for an increasing number of industrial products. The research and development investment which lies behind this scale of manufacture and the trading network essential to the achievement of effective sales volume demand an international scale of operation.

At the heart of all this development lies the need for communication: scientific, technological and commercial. Knowledge in all these spheres is expanding explosively and it must be disseminated, nationally and internationally. As new sciences are born, new technologies are created to serve them, and these in turn throw off splinters which become complete new sections of industry. Inevitably the need for specialist information grows.

The methods, skills and resources needed to acquire, process and disseminate this information are themselves the subject of extremely rapid growth and diversification. Among the many means that contribute to the spreading of knowledge the biggest and most dynamic is the trade and technical, or business, press.

This is an inadequate description of a complex branch of publishing whose purpose, over-simplified, might be described as follows: the *technical* journal is concerned with the making of the product (and the product can be anything from a toothbrush to a nuclear power station). The *trade* journal deals with the distribution, merchandising and servicing of the product. This branch of publishing also covers the service industries and includes professional and specialised journals. The former serve doctors, architects, lawyers, etc., and there is at least one for almost every profession. Specialised journals include the partly technical magazines dealing with a wide variety of interests; motoring, photography, yachting; tapering off in technical content until they merge with the consumer press.

Britain has long been regarded as the world leader in trade and technical publishing. This is not surprising in a country which initiated the industrial revolution and has always been one of the world's greatest trading nations. The trade and technical press fulfills an essential function in industry and commerce; it was born with it and remains an integral part of its whole operation and development.

There are in Britain some 200 publishers in the field producing a little over 2000 publications. This total has been growing at a rough annual average of between fifty and sixty titles during, e.g. the past twenty years or more. The make-up of the total is changing equally rapidly as journals are born, merged or quietly put to sleep as their usefulness ends. This is the corollary of a publishing service so closely geared to the pulse of industry. The trend is upward because industry and commerce are developing at a continually accelerating rate, both in size and in their need for specialized information.

The total circulation of these 2000 titles is substantially in excess of ten million copies, and total readership is four or five times that number. They serve industry, government and the professions in two ways because there are two markets—the reader in search of information and the advertiser in search of sales. All the technical progress in the world is of no avail unless the resulting end products can be sold and put to use. These two markets provide the publishers' sources of revenue, with much the bigger proportion coming from the sale of advertising space.

Oversimplifying again: those which flourish are those whose editorial content is most beneficial to readers in the branch of industry they serve. The publication stands or falls on the information it provides, its accuracy, relevance and authority, and in the ease and clarity with which it is presented.

The editorial staffs are not ordinary journalists. They are often scientists and technologists and are always specialists in the industries they serve. They travel widely and through training, concentrated study and involvement at all industrial levels they become impartial, comparative and analytical in outlook. Their accumulated, highly specialised knowledge and privileged access to industry allows informed and interpretative reporting which often amounts to valuable market research of a product and evaluation of a new process or a whole new technology.

Information, ideas, analysis, comparison and interpretation; that in outline is the service each publication seeks to provide for its own specified readership, and it is not perhaps surprising that in such an atmosphere advertisements are found to have special relevance and impact. For this reason the successful trade and technical journal has become a unique sales weapon for the industrial advertiser: the most effective medium by which a clearly defined and receptive market can be reached.

Industry Served	Percentage of total circulation outside U.K.
Aviation	46%
Chemistry & Chemicals	66%
Iron & Steel	51%
Mining	85%
Nucleonics	85%
Petroleum	45%
Plastics	31%
Shipping and Marine	54%

Table 23.1 Trade and technical press, circulation outside UK

This precise market penetration and receptive readership of the British trade and technical press is not confined to the United Kingdom (see Table 23.1). Readership is worldwide, and Britain exports a higher proportion of its publications than any other country. The overall percentage of 15.5 per cent of the ten million-plus circulation is in itself reasonably high but, when one examines the statistics of the leading journals in just a few key industries, the value placed on British trade and technical journals by overseas readers becomes apparent.

This world readership has arisen partly from a deliberate export policy by the trade and technical publishers, but there is more to it than just good salesmanship. The whole British economy is dependent upon world trade and international involvcment in scientific, technological and commercial developmcnt. It is natural, therefore, that the contents of its trade and technical press should be unusually international in coverage and outlook. If one adds to this an appreciation of the inventive skill which is perhaps Britain's greatest industrial asset, this degree of world readership will be readily understood.

24 Industrial press advertising

NORMAN A. HART

Norman Hart MSc, MCAM, Dip M, FIPR has specialised in the field of industrial communications and is now Director of Communication Advertising and Marketing (CAM) Education Foundation. An international lecturer and writer on industrial advertising and marketing, he is author of the most recent book on the subject, Industrial Publicity, *an Institute of Marketing approved text-book, and the* Glossary of Marketing Terms. *He holds a Masters Degree in Business Administration and is a Visiting Fellow of Bradford University.*

This chapter is an extract from the new edition of his *Industrial Advertising and Publicity* (Associated Business Press, 1978).

Press advertising in the industrial sector has come in for a good deal of criticism on the grounds of its ineffectiveness, relative to the large sums of money spent on it. Much of this has arisen from the inadequacy and inaccuracy of media selection and the incompetence of some advertisement design and copywriting. Often the failure, however, is traceable to different reasons, namely that the purpose of advertising has not been defined in advance or, if it has, it has been lost sight of.

For example, there is the sales manager's view when he sees some tens of thousands of pounds being spent on press advertising and relates this to the number of additional salesmen he could put on the road for such an expenditure. If, however, the purposes of these two channels of persuasion have been pre-defined, the one to provide active sales leads, the other to clinch the sale, they become mutually dependent and not competing alternatives.

The position of press advertising within the broad communications framework must be established at the outset, and its strengths and weaknesses analysed. In comparison with a salesman who can influence, say, five or six persons a day, a publication can reach thousands or indeed millions of people in the same time. The message in an advertisment must necesarily be shorter and the percentage of readers upon whom the message will have any impact may be of low order, but the impact can be increased by various devices such as the number of appearances, size of space and so on. A salesman, to be effective, must first find his prospect and then secure an interview. With an advertisement this is not necessary: prospects need only be defined in general terms and a publication by virtue of its blanket circulation will ensure a large coverage of a potential market. The cost of delivering a particular message is also relevant since for a salesman it may amount to several pounds per contact whereas for an advertisement only a few pence.

Recent research in the USA[1] showed that the cost per sales call was standing at $71.27 in 1975, and rising at a rate approximating to double that of advertising space. Figure 24.1 shows the trend.

In order to make a comparison with press advertising, another piece of American research has been taken[2], and here a sales call, estimated at $50, compares with an 'advertising

1. McGraw Hill Research Report 8013.3.
2. US Steel/Harnisachteger Study, American Business Press.

contact' at around 10-15 cents.

Whilst these data relate to the American market, it should not be difficult for any advertiser to produce his own figures in relation to his own company. From McGraw-Hill however an intercomparison has been made as between all European markets, and on the most recent research available, the cost per sales call in the UK (1975) averaged out at $27 which at the time converted into £13. The range of costs from which this figure was obtained stretched from £3 to £38 covering all sectors of industrial selling.

The usefulness of press advertising must now be examined in more detail, and in particular it should be assessed against its specific purpose, that is, the defined job to be done. It is useful to list each of the factors involved to see where press advertising fits into the overall picture:

Size of market: the larger the market and the greater the number of potential buying influences (referred to as decision-making units—DMUs) the greater the efficiency of press advertising. If some thousands of people are involved, press advertising will be efficient, if only hundreds it may be marginal, and if less than that it is probably of little use. Only a fraction of a publication's readership will take notice of a single appearance of an advertisement, and a readership is rarely more than a fraction of a potential market.

Impact: there is little doubt that the average impact value of an advertisement is low. That is to say, the percentage of total audience who are able to recall the advertising message is usually only a few per cent. This is where creativity—the creative expression of the selling message—has its part to play. The impact value of an advertisement can be increased by repetition and the number of publications it appears in.

Selling message: this must necessarily be restricted both for reasons of space available and also because the length of the selling message tends to operate in inverse proportion to impact, i.e. the shorter the message, the greater the chance that it will be read.

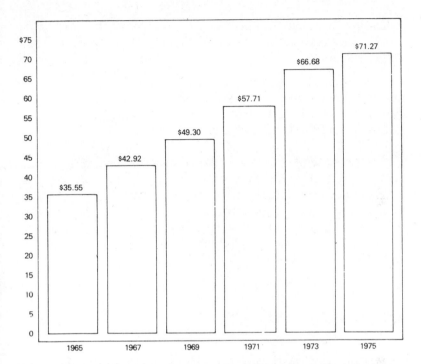

Figure 24.1 Increase in cost of industrial sales calls, USA

Penetration: by virtue of the pass-on readership of a journal a sales message can be expected to penetrate further into and amongst decision-making units than most other forms of publicity, including the sales force.

Intrusion: since a person reads an advertisement only if he wishes (in fact an intrinsic weakness) it follows that he will experience little sense of intrusion upon his time. He is therefore in a receptive, enquiring frame of mind, or at least neutral.

Speed: with daily newspapers an advertisement can be produced and inserted in a matter of a few days. As most industrial advertising is concerned with weekly or monthly journals a much more normal time is three to six weeks, allowing for design and production. Although this is not very rapid, once produced it can cover a very large audience for a long time.

Cost: Even allowing for the considerable communications inefficiency already mentioned, press advertising in the UK tends to be the cheapest medium at cost per potential customer, particularly for large audiences.

The purpose of press advertising therefore is to play its part in the overall marketing mix having regard to its cost effectiveness in relation to the other channels of persuasion. It is not so much a question of selecting only the medium having the highest cost effectiveness, since each will have its own basic limitations; rather it is a matter of establishing a mixture which in total will have the greatest effect.

Effectiveness

In *How British Industry Buys*[3], respondents to a questionnaire indicated that advertisements in the trade press had a relatively small part to play in providing information which influenced the purchase of industrial products. The highest category was 'operating management' of whom thirty-two per cent cited press advertising as one of the two most important channels of communication. Perhaps the most important category, board members, scored only fourteen per cent.

There is good evidence in this survey that respondents are not always willing to admit even to themselves what the are outside factors they allow to influence them in reaching purchasing decisions. Sales engineers' visits for instance were rated at sixty-six per cent by board members, yet elsewhere in the survey only eighteen per cent of board members ever saw

3. Hugh Buckner, *How British Industry Buys*, Hutchinson, London, 1967.

a sales engineer! Since the first figure is an expression of opinion and the latter one of fact, eighteen per cent is more likely to be the accurate figure. If not from sales engineers, where did board members obtain the information upon which to make decisions? Advertising may well in fact deserve a higher rating than these respondents were prepared to admit.

In the USA a good deal of work has been done to relate on a very broad basis the effectiveness of press advertising to sales.

A survey published by McGraw-Hill[4] shows that of 893 industrial companies, when the ratio of advertising to selling expense, i.e. advertising plus direct selling costs (salesmen's salaries, commission, travel and entertainment), is higher, the ratio of selling expense to sales turnover is lower. On average it was found that 'high advertisers' (where advertising accounted for more than twenty per cent of selling expense) had a twenty-one per cent lower overall selling cost than 'low advertisers'. The trend was found to be consistent regardless of the volume of sales and of product groups. In the former case, 'high' advertisers in each of four sales size groups had average selling expense sixteen to thirteen per cent lower than the 'low' advertisers.

For the machinery group (all special industrial machinery such as machine tools and construction machinery, motors, instruments and controls, transport and communications equipment) the sales expense ratio was twenty-five per cent lower on average among 'high' advertisers than among 'low' advertisers.

For the materials group (raw materials and ingredients such as steel, industrial chemicals, rubber and plastics, structural products) the difference was twenty-seven per cent. For the equipment supplies group (maintenance and operating supplies such as furniture, paper products, lubicants, tyres, valves, machine tool accessories, paint, lighting fixtures, electronic components) the difference was fifteen per cent.

4. McGraw-Hill, *How Advertising Affects the Cost of Selling*, London, 1963.

There are wide differences in the amount of investment in industrial advertising even amongst firms in the same industry. This is only to be expected but it is unfortunate that the reasons for such differences are often subjective or illogical. They are sometimes based on a philosophy of 'I don't believe in advertising', a comment which has as much rational background as not believing in raw materials. Or perhaps the sales manager thinks he knows exactly who his customers are and calls upon them at frequent intervals—a proposition which can almost always be disproved on methodical investigation.

The final effectiveness of advertising for a company must be judged on the merits of each case. Two authoritative observers of its role as a reinforcement to personal selling in the industrial field comment, 'Many salesmen and managers completely underrate the importance of corroborative function of industrial advertising. Because they may not be able to point to sales or worthwhile prospects obtained by advertising they assume that their advertising is not effective. In fact however a company's generalised reputation is most important; and although advertising is only one factor in building up this reputation it is a vital one.'[5]

Cost effectiveness

The cost per thousand total circulation basis, so popular with publishers, is quite inadequate for effective media assessment. Equally unrealistic as a rule is cost per order originating from a given journal, since the number of traceable contracts are usually of such a low order as to be statistically unreliable.

Cost per reader within the defined marketing group is probably the most effective basis of assessing a publication, though in some instances cost per enquiry can be an even

5. David Rowe and Ivan Alexander, *Selling of Industrial Products,* Hutchinson, London, 1968, p. 96.

better guide. This latter factor necessarily depends on whether enquiries are what an advertisement is designed to achieve. A study of packaging media for instance showed the cost per thousand circulation to vary little as between one publication and another. When the required readership for a particular pack was examined, the cost per reader varied from £1.5 per thousand to £20 per thousand. Moreover, after the top two publications had been added together, further additions made no significant difference to the number of readers reached. In this instance it was found possible to reduce the number of publications from eight to two, increase the concentration and level of advertising, and thus impact, whilst at the same time reducing expenditure.

Circulation and advertising rates

When the overall economics of publishing are considered it is generally found that advertising rates of British publications are reasonably geared to production costs. Within any specialised sector it is usual to find the forces of competition have caused the cost per thousand copies of one journal to be much the same as another. Indeed so far as the absolute level of cost per page is concerned it might be argued that the rates tend to be too low to enable a publisher to provide a good enough all round service to maximise the marketing efficiency of his publication.

The important differences between rates begin to emerge only when readership 'segmentation' is considered and here the advertiser is at a great disadvantage. Accurate and authentic data on total circulations are beginning to emerge, but circulation breakdowns are usually no more than a publisher's statement and the bitter fact is that these must be treated with reserve. Until circulation breakdowns are subject to independent audit it is unwise to pay any serious regard to them since the basis on which they are compiled is unknown and they cannot be subject to comparative study.

Given the difficulty of determining cost/readership effectiveness, there are still opportunities for significant savings on the basis of rates alone. For instance, in determining how many publications to place on a schedule in relation to how many insertions in each, graduated scales of charges are worth examining since quantity reductions in page rates can effect major economies. Long-term contracts can enable further savings to be made, and notwithstanding the existence of published rate cards, many publishers are prepared to negotiate prices in order to increase their share of business.

A growing trend amongst publishers is to offer discount rates based on the total business placed in certain groups of publications. Another variation is to consider financial concessions related to the time of year.

An alternative to looking for special rate reductions is to look for special services from a publisher. There are many facilities which can be placed at the disposal of an advertiser which will help to make his campaign more effective. Progressive publishers are recognising this and are prepared to co-operate, for instance in split runs, inserts, and joint research. One questionable service is the occasional offer of editorial preference in consideration of the placing of advertising. If a journal is willing to do business on this basis it can only mean that it is prepared to forfeit its editorial independence in order to make short-term gains at the expense of the reader and therefore the advertiser.

An interesting term in the publishing business is the 'numbers game'. It is a reflection on the gullibility of some advertisers that the journal most likely to be chosen as number one on a schedule is that having the greatest circulation. Before the introduction of free circulation journals, this might have been a valid criterion in an homogeneous market, but where it represents, as is now sometimes the case, simply an expression of the print order, its claims are quite misleading.

Over the past decade a large number of publications have appeared, almost always given away, with circulation methods which are sometimes not controlled with any degree of effectiveness. Such journals have had circulations inflated by a factor first of two, then three and then four—each publisher going one better in quoting a higher number. Rates for such journals expressed in relation to circulation totals have seemed reasonable, but any company librarian will quote example after example of the inflow of duplicate copies of such journals which serve to benefit the printer, papermaker and publisher, but not the advertiser.

In numerous readership surveys there is ample evidence of magazines quoting massive circulation figures but receiving extraordinarily low readership ratings. The moral, as always, is let the buyer beware, and verify all facts by independent audit.

25 'If it's worth having, it's worth paying for'

or 'Why I'd like you to believe in subscription magazines'

JAMES BENN

James Benn graduated from Cambridge with an engineering degree in 1965, and spent some months as a journalist with United Press International's Rome Bureau. He continued his training with Southam Business Press in Toronto before joining Benn's finally in January 1967. He successively managed one monthly magazine, published three, directed five and since January 1977 has been in charge of Benn Publications Limited, the subsidiary of Benn Brothers responsible for all trade magazines and directories.

I am a convert. Like all converts, I cannot wait to bring everyone else into the faith.

The faith? Paid circulation magazines, subscription magazines.

It all started in the post strike. My conversion, that is. 'Organise copy deliveries in London and surrounding major towns' they said. 'Priority for the weeklies, of course, but if you can get some monthlies to subscribers, so much the better'.

Luckily a whole lot of people in our company knew London a great deal better than I, and luckier still, a few of them had some idea how to organise a basically military exercise. Best of all we had a staff quite prepared to down typewriters and form two-man teams with our 'wheelmen', the ad sales and editorial staff, and spend two days a week delivering journals.

It worked. After an initial ten days hiatus, most subscribers to Benn publications in London and surrounding towns like Croydon, Luton and Slough began getting deliveries of their trade magazines. Something similar happened on a much smaller scale in Birmingham and Manchester. We only managed thirty per cent of normal circulation, but it was still a proportion that no other publisher achieved.

And my conversion? On Slough Trading Estate.

I cannot remember which particular subscriber it was, or even which magazine we got to him that day. It probably wasn't any one event but the cumulative effect of hearing people's heartfelt thanks when they, left without their twice daily fix of incoming mail, suddenly, out of the blue, were handed the latest issue of their chosen trade magazine. No addict could have expressed greater relief, greater joy. And the combined effect of ten or fifteen identical expressions profoundly impressed me.

These businessmen, these subscribers, genuinely relied on their trade magazine to help them run their business. Whether it was news, company information, or warnings read from the page of the latest county court judgements, whether they were big companies, or little, their trade magazine was essential to them. And brother, did they come clean and tell us so!

All of which may be completely obvious to the readers of *ADMAP*. But it certainly was not to me, fresh from a training period working for another business magazine publisher in North America. Over there they were totally into controlled circulation. And so, until revelation came on Slough Trading Estate, was I.

But conversion has its problems. A believer in subscription journals is essentially a schizophrenic. At least if the publications carry advertising. In Benn's case, around seventy-five per cent of our trade publications' income is from the advertiser, leaving reader income very much as the minority revenue source. And a far from easy revenue source at that. Subscription promotion is a very painstaking, detailed, low-return and time-consuming operation, and any magazine manager would prefer to spend that time selling advertising space, simply because subscription promotion work is never going to give the equivalent satisfaction of landing a £10000 advertisement order. But if you believe in subscription journals, the work has to be done.

A controlled circulation publisher has a much simpler life. To him the business audience of his magazine is just another part of the package he is putting together to sell. Working backwards, having decided his target advertisers, he can precisely identify their customers, do his desk research and put together the best possible list as his circulation base. Admittedly, the names change, companies come and go, but the publisher can always make sure he is sending copies to a pretty complete audience.

Set against this, the subscription journal publisher often seems a blundering amateur. He cannot possibly deliver a neat and tidy audience. On one side too many accountants in too many companies decide that their divisional managers do not need so many magazines. On the other, fringe readers are always flitting in from somewhere to add to the subscription income, but to be of little use to an advertiser.

CC is tidy, efficient and saleable. And I, having seen only that in North America, had thought nothing could touch it. But I had not reckoned on that great intangible that paid journals have...their extraordinarily intimate relationship with the subscriber.

When a hard-headed businessman pays good money for a journal, he is going to read it. Take *ADMAP*. No-one pays over £2 an issue just because his companions on the 07.36 recognise it as a status symbol. They don't. Yet he pays. There must be something in it. So with all paid magazines. Having paid his money he is going to read it. It may be a nuisance, sitting in his briefcase for two or three commuter journeys before he gets around to it...but get around to it he will, and then he will take the time to read it. Our latest figures indicate a very high proportion of readership at home.

It is a totally different attitude from that of the recipient of a CC journal. It is that difference that ensures the advertiser's message is reaching the audience when he is ready to take it in.

Attitudes, however, are hardly best expressed by a self-confessed convert to one particular cause. They need properly and independently researching. They need tabulating. They need verifying...but most of all they need publicising. And that is one thing that no T & T subscription journal publisher has been doing sufficiently.

Trade magazine publishers, constantly admonished by the agencies for their lack of readership data, spend more and more money proving that their circulation gives good market coverage. That their magazine is thought more of than someone else's. That, yes, the readers do check through the ads. That 4.3 people read every copy. We have all been concentrating on numbers. Here the publisher is on familiar ground, battling it out with his friendly (?) neighbourhood rival. But get him on to emotions and he is lost. Pity, because that is the ground on which he has most to win, once he can establish that it is not just the numbers that matter.

Research and Marketing Developments Limited, on behalf of Benn Publications carried out a dip-stick survey into attitudes to the trade press in 1977. Their findings were used for the basis for our report *The Trade Press in Britain*. From this for the first time, we had a comparison with other media, not just other trade magazines, and to no publisher's surprise (but maybe to some advertisers?) we found that nine out of ten chief executives interviewed rated the trade press as their most important source of business information. That

overlapped with four out of ten who rated the national press
as their most important source. Nine against four. The
nationals cannot hold a candle to us. Add to this the separate
figures which all publishers can supply on how many people
read each copy, and their job titles, and two startlingly clear
facts emerge...*How British Industry Buys* should have been
put together by the trade press not by a national paper; and
the prime route to any 'decision making unit' must be
through subscribed-for trade journals.

American Business Press, the trade organisation of
business magazine publishers in the US, spends a great deal
of its income researching and promoting the trade press. In
many ways they are ahead of us. In one, however, they are
behind. Controlled circulation is still very much the
publishing norm in North America. But things are changing.
Even they have realised that numbers are not everything.
Results are what matters. And there is one magazine whose
success as a paid publication is bringing the message right
home to them. *FOLIO,* 'the magazine for magazine
management' started publication in June 1972. Everyone was
very excited about it then and people still feel passionately
about it now. They read it from cover to cover, they mark up
sections and send copies around drawing the particular
attention of key people to different articles. FOLIO is a paid-
for publication. Within two years of launching the magazine,
Joe Hanson decided he had got the right product and sent out
a series of ever tougher ultimatums. 'Pay or no more copies'.
They paid, and now it is paying for *FOLIO*'s advertisers too.

Have I converted you? Have I even aroused the slightest
curiosity?

I could have filled the article with numbers, quoted this
source and that, and got thoroughly bogged down in abstract
argument. There is only one way of convincing you that
subscription journals are best (and that T & T are the best
business media) and that is by letting you convince yourself
by doing your own research. Perhaps one interview would
do. An interview with yourself. Is there any magazine you
receive for free at home or at work, which you pay the same

attention to as one you pay for?
  Subscription journals rule...OK?

26   Controlled circulation

G.R. PARVIN

G.R. Parvin is a Director of IPC Business Press (Sales and Distribution) Ltd., and a member of the Council of the Audit Bureau of Circulations.

Like many other aspects of modern life which we suppose to be recent innovations, controlled circulation, as a method of distribution for trade and technical journals is, in fact, much older than it appears. One of the leading engineering publications in the United States with a circulation running into many thousands was first published in 1894. The distribution is controlled and has been for so many years that nobody is now quite sure whether it was actually launched with controlled distribution or changed to this system after launch.

In Budapest, Hungary, in the late 1920s, *Machinery Lloyd* was launched with a controlled distribution on an international scale—and this paper still exists.

According to the *Audit Notes and Instructions for Publishers and Auditors,* issued by the Audit Bureau of Circulations, controlled circulation is defined as follows:

'This must consist solely of single copies sent free

and post frcc to individuals who precisely fit the Terms of Control.'

The *Notes* then go on to define Terms of Control as follows:

'... (they) must be published in each issue of the journal and must specify separately the industrial, commercial or professional classifications covered by the journal and the job qualifications required to qualify for receipt of a copy of the journal.'

These definitions embody the basic principles of modern controlled circulation in this country. The *Notes* then go on to define fairly rigidly the two main types of controlled circulation, i.e. requested circulation and non-requested circulation. Taken as a whole, they form a comparatively strict set of rules governing controlled distribution.

But it was not always so.

Shortly after the last war American journals enjoying controlled distribution blossomed in considerable numbers, but the majority of them contained little or no editorial matter, and what there was consisted mainly of public relations hand-outs—from manufacturers. They were sent uninvited to lists of names and addresses which were sometimes of dubious quality. But a number of them prospered; and the idea spread across the Atlantic, as ideas often do, and by the early 1950s such journals were being launched in the United Kingdom with great frequency. Again, they consisted of paste-ups of manufacturers' hand-outs with as much advertising space as could be sold, and were despatched to as many names as the advertisements would pay for and leave a profit for the publisher. In some cases publishers would send large numbers of copies to each address on their list in order to claim the maximum circulation. Other dubious practices were rife at that time and it is this period which gave controlled circulation, as a method of distribution, a bad name which it has taken a number of years to live down.

Nevertheless, reputable publishers could see that here was a type of distribution which had a place in publishing and which could be of value to industry and publisher alike, but that it was being abused. Yet despite this, it was sometimes successful enough to threaten some of the old-established paid circulation journals. A number of established publishers decided to enter this field themselves, but to do so on legitimate terms.

By the late 1950s journals began to appear which made claims to a high proportion of requested readership. This was one of the first efforts to qualify contolled circulation readership in addition to quantifying it. It had been found that readers did not object to giving quite an amount of information about their companies and themselves in return for a free journal which was of use to them.

The journals which had a high proportion of readers who had completed an application form specifically requesting that the journal be sent to them, enjoyed a more effective circulation than those which were sent out entirely uninvited to recipients; although it is important to mention that there were, and still are, some exceptions to this rule.

However, an investigation conducted in my own company around this time analysing reader enquiries, showed that on most journals with controlled distributions, three times as many enquiries per thousand readers were received from requested readers as from non-requested readers.

By 1962 the situation had, to a large extent, settled down and an examination of the membership of the Audit Bureau of Circulations Trade and Technical section for that year shows that out of 324 member journals, 120, i.e. thirty-seven per cent, had the majority of their circulation listed as free or unpaid. This was the equivalent of controlled circulation at that time, since there was no official classification for controlled circulation in the Audit Bureau statistics.

An analysis of the Audit Bureau of Circulations Review Serial No. 90, July–December 1976, is shown in Table 26.1 From this it emerges that in 1962 and in 1976, the percentage of journals with a controlled circulation element in their distribution was exactly the same.

But why controlled circulation?

Satisfactory advertisement revenues are vital to trade and technical publications. With their comparatively small circulations they can never hope to exist on circulation revenue. Very often the advertiser wishes to reach a specialised market, or to cover a particular section completely, and to have no waste circulation. A successful controlled circulation journal serving the area that the advertiser wishes to reach can offer him this facility. The Terms of Control specify the industries or areas of activity to be covered and the occupations of individuals within those areas who are qualified to become readers. All applications are checked to ensure that they fall within the Terms of Control and therefore in relation to these Terms there is not waste circulation.

Furthermore, in many cases the journal can claim to reach almost every individual, or at least every establishment, within the Terms of Control. This it is extremely difficult for a paid circulation journal to achieve. Also a controlled

Analysis of journals by method of distribution.

	No.	%
Journals making returns	516	100
Journals with CC element	192	37 (but issue 41% of MDFs)
Journals non-optional Society etc.	130	25
Total not specifically purchased	322	62

Table 26.1 ABC Review Serial No. 90, July-December 1976

circulation journal, vigorously promoted to its potential readership, can reach this situaiton very rapidly after launching. It can take a paid circulation years to achieve nothing more than a fair coverage of the same field.

From the publisher's point of view, the acquisition of duly qualified requested readers can often be achieved at less than one-tenth the cost of acquiring a new paid reader. Additionally, the fact that information about each reader and his organisation has been secured, enables comprehensive analyses of the distribution to be presented to advertisers. Although it is perhaps somewhat surprising that despite the fact that journals with a controlled circulation element in their distribution account for thirty-seven per cent of the ABC trade and technical membership, they account for only forty-one per cent of the Media Data Forms issued or to be issued.

Of course not all the facts are on the side of controlled distribution. Since the entire circulation is normally distributed by post, postal rates are a key factor in their economics. Increases in these rates bear heavily on the publishers. These journals are also vulnerable to the effects of inflation upon print, paper and editorial costs—particularly since most successful controlled circulation journals now have as high an editorial standard as any paid circulation journal. From the publisher's point of view, this means that if the journal is not successful it can quickly accumulate large losses.

There is another expensive area which often appertains to the controlled circulation journal, and that is the reader enquiry service, or *Bingo* cards. The more successful the journal is in producing enquiries to be channelled through the publisher to the manufacturer or supplier, the greater the expense in which the publisher becomes involved and all of these costs must be met from the advertisement revenue. Yet there is, of course a constant struggle to keep the advertisement rates competitive with paid circulation rivals.

One spin-off from the controlled circulation journal, which is perhaps a more lucrative operation for the publisher than the normal reader enquiry service, is the *product card* or *product information service*. This is a form of communal direct mail sent to the distribution list of a controlled circulation journal, or to a selection from the list. Being composed solely of perforated sheets of business reply cards, each one addressed to the manufacturer—whose product is featured on the reverse of the address side and on the stub of the card—it involves no further expense for the publisher and directs enquiries back to the manufacturer.

These publications do have a disadvantage in that whereas two or three of the *Bingo* cards are inserted in a single copy of the journal, normally only one of the reply paid cards is included in the product information booklet. Consequently, when the first reader has detached and despatched the card to the manufacturer, subsequent readers find it more difficult to make enquiries. Nevertheless, a number of these publications enjoy considerable support from advertisers and produce very satisfactory results.

And what of the future? We have seen that although between 1962 and 1977 costs of all kinds have risen dramatically, the percentage of trade and technical journals distributed by the controlled circulation method has remained almost exactly the same. The reason undoubtedly is that a successful controlled circulation journal can be profitable to both advertiser and publisher alike. An unsuccessful one dies quickly.

It is very doubtful whether the titles that made up the thirty-seven per cent in 1962 are the same on the whole as the titles that make up the current thirty-seven per cent. What does seem to be evident however, is that there is always room for the good idea for a new controlled circulation journal. It can either create its own market or force its way into an existing market place and prosper.

There are signs that the new journals appearing in the trade and technical field are dividing themselves into two major classes. The first is the controlled circulation journal and the second is the high priced, highly technical, limited circulation journal, which does not rely upon advertising for its main source of revenue. This could very well be the pattern, in general, for the future in this field.

27 Britain's publishing strength in the trade and technical press

BRIAN GRIFFIN

Chairman, Building (Publishers) Ltd.

In my office at Builder House stands a small replica of a hansom cab. This is a constant reminder that *The Builder* was founded by the Victorian architect and designer Joseph Aloysius Hansom, designer of the original hansom cab. It is also a constant reminder of how well established is the trade and technical press in this country, for *The Builder* came into being in 1842.

Nor is it the oldest. I can bring to mind *New Law Journal* (1822) and *The Lancet* (1823) as earlier survivors from that era. The publishing strength of the trade and technical press is deep rooted in a country which led the world in industrialisation, throwing up at the same time the need for new communication links in specialist fields. And being deep rooted, it has a sure growth. Today there are some 2300 titles listed in British Rate and Data, covering more than 200 professional business and industrial categories, to the envy of the rest of the publishing world.

Growth has been particularly fast over the last 20 years. Certainly as far as the construction sector was concerned, the spur was the lucrative advertising markets which opened up as the large redevelopment programme got fully into its stride in the late 1950s and early 1960s. Manufacturers of building products, materials and systems had unprecedented amounts of money to spend to bring their products before the eyes of the people they most wished to reach, the specifiers. The architectural and building press, alive to what was happening, responded by advancements in every aspect of their publishing operations, better editorial, services, and marketing, to increase their attractions as media for the advertising appropriations.

A similar surge was experienced in other industries as demand increased with disposable income and heavy investments were at last released in new technologies, research and development and product innovation. Each established field of specialist interest became a potential area of publishing interest, thanks to the voracious reading habits of the British public, the ingenuity and drive of British publishing houses and the explosive expansion of knowledge in science, commerce and technology.

Recent valuable research by Benn Publications Limited *(The Trade Press in Britain)* reveals that there are now some 639 publications produced by 76 publishers in the category of what they define as the trade press in Britain. This compares with only 342 publications from 49 publishers some 20 years ago.

By the same token there has been a decrease in the number of titles since 1966, and in the number of publishers. But the sixties saw an over-rapid growth in new titles, since when many have been merged or put to sleep. This is the symptom of an industry so closely matched to the rapidly changing needs of its readership. The trend of real growth remains strong, despite the soaring production costs of the last few years which have led to large scale rationalisations. IPC Business Press remains the country's leading trade publisher with 103 titles, of which half belong to the Audit Bureau of

Publisher	Total Titles	Total ABC-Titles	Combined ABC Circulation
IPC Business Press	102	63	1,216,466
Morgan-Grampian	24	23	427,864
Haymarket Group	14	8(9)	346,653
Thomson Organisation	27	20	337,373
Benn Publications	31	28	212,917
Maclean Hunter	18	15	203,049
Mercury House	16	7	162,274
Maclaren Publishers	11	10	126,509
William Reed	5	3	78,170
Industrial Newspapers	19	13	47,510

Source: "The Trade Press in Britain"—Benn Publications, 1977.

Table 27.1 Leading trade press publishers' titles and ABC circulations, 1977

Circulation (with combined circulation in excess of 1.2 million). Second largest by size of combined ABC circulation is Morgan Grampian, followed by Haymarket, the Thomson Organisation and Benn Publications (see Table 27.1). Aside from the top ten, the remaining 368 titles are published by a variety of houses, some small, others miniscule.

It emerges then that the publication of trade and technical journals is in the hands of two distinct categories of organisation: the big battalions, with a publication in every aspect of industry that is viable, and the smaller organisations specialising in their own particular fields. There is no doubt that some of these smaller houses produce a product that is invaluable to both the reader and the advertiser, and the end product is a highly professional package.

The trade press now ranks as the number one source of information on specific industries. The features, news and statistics published are regularly applied as a tool of the trade or filed away for future reference. It is read at home as well as in the office, laboratory, factory or site. Publishers have sufficient confidence in the product to increase the percentage of trade press titles covered by the Audit Bureau of Circulation from 24.9 per cent in 1956 to 80.9 per cent in 1976. Through the Audit Bureau of Circulation (ABC), British publishers provide advertisers and their agents with a far higher proportion of independently authenticated circulation data than any other press in the world.

And advertisers have got the message. Trade and technical advertising expenditure has increased by something like two-thirds since 1972; magazines and periodicals in general have gone up by a half since then. That is growth, absolute and comparative.

Advertising is of course, of the essence. Against a background of editorial information, ideas, interpretation and commentary, advertisements have a special power and impact. So the trade and technical press not only have a perceptive readership but also a sharp market penetration. And this can be international too. Happily, English is still by far the principal commercial language throughout the world. Britain exports a higher proportion of its publications than any other country; a tribute not only to the marketing drive of our publishers, but also to the widely based British involvement in world trade and international development in scientific, technological and commercial affairs. But it has not all been freewheeling growth. Trade and technical journals were for a long time, and with some justification, accused of not providing their prospective advertisers with sufficient details of their own readership or the market place that they served. Unlike the national press they were usually unable to give a great wealth of information on the spending (or buying) powers of their readers.

In recent years, and closely related to the advent of the controlled circulation journals, more and more research has been carried out by independent organisations funded by a group of competitive journals, or by sophisticated in-house research which is acceptable to advertisers and their agents. Research is an expensive marketing tool, and in the past publishers had felt that unless the ends justified the means, in other words more advertising space, they were not prepared to enter into it. Advertising rates had always been low in the trade and technical press and one had to sell a lot of space to pay for a piece of research.

Times have changed though, rates have become more realistic, and in areas of industry where there are several successful and competitive journals there is nearly always good research available to the media buyer. Much detailed information on editorial policy, geographical distribution, specifying power related to circulation is now made available in the Media Data Form introduced by ABC in 1974. The ABC's Media Data Form (MDF) is likely to become the blueprint for similar standards of control that, it is hoped, will soon be created for use throughout western Europe. In reaching our industry buyers future exporters can safely rely on the ABC authenticated data set out on the MDFs of the trade and technical press in this country.

Business and professional readers in other countries are catered for by a mixture of subscription and controlled circulation titles. The situation in the UK, however, is uniquely different. Here, in addition to the above means of distribution, readers of the more established and successful periodicals enjoy the further option of purchasing their copies from newsagents. Nowhere else in the world is this such common practice and the value of these readers to advertisers is enormous. Consider the busy professional or executive who, week after week, calls at the newsagent, or has delivered, his chosen periodical to read at home. What better environment could be created in which to sell him data processing, doors or drawingboards? His commitment to that magazine in renewing his faith for each successive issue is possibly greater even than a subscriber. It is nevertheless true that publishers tend to underplay this element of their sales and perhaps because this is so, advertising agents are unaware of its considerable value. Newstrade sales are, by definition, hard to categorise specifically. The fact that they exist, however, should never be overlooked.

There is still a tremendous disparity in the rate structure of trade and technical journals. It is easy to look in the pages of BRAD and find a journal with a circulation of 2000 and a page rate of £195, and another with a circulation of 32000 and a page rate of £260. Circulation in itself has little to do with the rate card, penetration of the market has everything.

When one thinks of service, both to the reader and the advertiser, one cannot ignore the enquiry services which most product-orientated journals now provide. A reader requiring further information from an advertiser, or a group of advertisers, merely fills in a reply-paid card and details of the request are promptly forwarded to the advertisers concerned. Obviously this service can be abused by the literature-seeking reader, but advertisers rely to a great extent on the response that they achieve from this service, not only as a means for attracting business but also as a basis for planning future advertising schedules.

Advertisers and their agents are quite rightly demanding more and more information from the media owner and, if this pressure is kept up, and advertising is bought on these criteria, publishers will respond and the advertiser will benefit. It does seem inevitable, however, that to provide this service advertisement rates must be raised accordingly. The trade and technical press has made great editorial strides; shedding its complacency, it has adopted much more aggressive attitudes towards gathering news and interpreting events, and it is providing specialist services to its readers of a high degree of sophistication. It happens very frequently nowadays that the national press will repeat a story first used in a technical magazine, and specialist journalists from trade and technical magazines are being used for expert commentary increasingly on radio and television. Regular courses now exist for training journalists in this field. It remains a fact that the periodicals we publish are vitally concerned with the many trades and manufacturing techniques on which our economy is so dependent.

For those who have the confidence in their markets and in their editorial packages, the rewards are likely to be even greater than in the past. The trade and technical press is flexing its muscles, and is investing in the sort of quality that can only enhance its strength.

Index